The Baseball Handbook

Bernie Walter

Human Kinetics

Library of Congress Cataloging-in-Publication Data

Walter, Bernie, 1942-
    The baseball handbook / Bernie Walter.
      p. cm.
    ISBN 0-7360-3985-6
      1. Baseball--United States--Handbooks, manuals, etc. I. Title.

    GV880.4.W35 2002
    796.357'62--dc21

                                                                    2001039842

ISBN: 0-7360-3985-6

Acquisitions Editor: Todd Jensen; **Managing Editor:** Wendy McLaughlin; **Assistant Editors:** John
Wentworth, Dan Brachtesende; **Copyeditor:** Robert Replinger; **Proofreader:** Joanna Hatzopoulos
Portman; **Graphic Designer:** Robert Reuther; **Graphic Artists:** Kim Maxey, Tara Welsch; **Photo
Manager:** Tom Roberts; **Cover Designer:** Keith Blomberg; **Photographer (cover):** Tom Roberts;
Photographer (interior): Tom Roberts, unless otherwise noted; photos pp. iii, 21, 77: ©2002 Tom
Roberts Photography; **Art Manager:** Carl Johnson; **Illustrator:** Tom Roberts; **Printer:** United Graphics

Printed in the United States of America   10 9 8 7 6 5 4 3 2 1

Human Kinetics
Web site: www.humankinetics.com

United States: Human Kinetics, P.O. Box 5076, Champaign, IL 61825-5076
800-747-4457
e-mail: humank@hkusa.com

Canada: Human Kinetics, 475 Devonshire Road Unit 100, Windsor, ON N8Y 2L5
800-465-7301 (in Canada only)
e-mail: orders@hkcanada.com

Europe: Human Kinetics, Units C2/C3 Wira Business Park, West Park Ring Road
Leeds LS16 6EB, United Kingdom
+44 (0) 113 278 1708
e-mail: hk@hkeurope.com

Australia: Human Kinetics, 57A Price Avenue, Lower Mitcham, South Australia 5062
08 8277 1555
e-mail: liahka@senet.com.au

New Zealand: Human Kinetics, P.O. Box 105-231, Auckland Central
09-523-3462
e-mail: hkp@ihug.co.nz

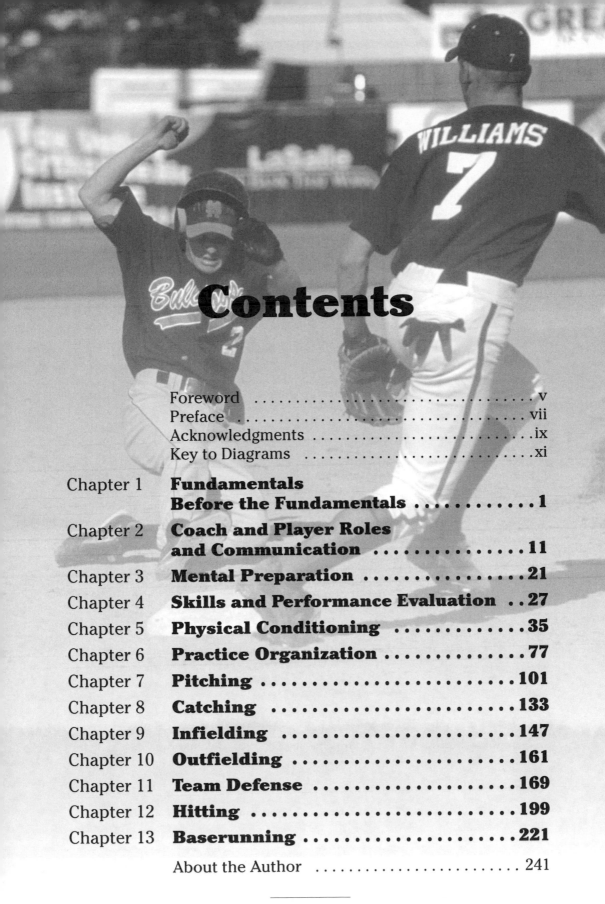

Contents

Foreword

When I arrived at Arundel High School, I was a skinny little kid with raw talent but limited knowledge of baseball. Then I met Coach Bernie Walter. Bernie's knowledge and passion for baseball was unmatched by anyone back then. Even today I'm not sure if I know anyone who knows more or cares more about the game than Bernie does.

Our team would have the longest practices, even when working on fielding or bunting. At the time I hated it, but looking back I see how much better it made my teammates and me. One of my most vivid memories is the day after we lost a game to our archrival, Old Mill High School. Our team had made four or five errors and plenty of other mistakes. Baseball practice the next day was the longest one yet. We performed infield and outfield drills the entire time. If any of us made an error or a mistake, the entire team had to sprint from our positions to the left foul pole, to the right foul pole, and then back to our positions. From that day on I hated to lose with an unbelievable passion.

In this book you will learn all the techniques that I learned from Coach Walter, techniques that I still execute today—pitching mechanics, bunt defenses, the correct way to run the bases, and simply how to outsmart the opponent. Whatever you're looking for, it's in this book. I believe that every player or coach will get something out of this book.

I have many people to thank for helping me reach the major leagues, but none more than Coach Walter. He taught me the correct way to play baseball, not only physically but also mentally. I doubt that I will ever find a way to thank Bernie enough for what he did for me.

Denny Neagle, *Colorado Rockies*

Preface

In my first year at the University of Maryland, a professor asked the people in my class to raise our hands if we were there to learn how to teach. Few of us raised our hands. Then he asked, "How many of you have come to learn how to coach?" Nearly everyone in the class raised their hands. The professor told us that to be a great coach, you had to be a great teacher first. He challenged us to observe coaches and teachers carefully and critically and to emulate their good characteristics. That has been my goal throughout my career as a teacher and coach.

I have experience as a player; as an assistant coach at the college, high school, and USA Baseball levels; and as an instructor in minor league training camps. Through these experiences I have had the unique opportunity to study coaches and players from amateur to professional levels. *The Baseball Handbook* is a compilation of what I have learned through careful observation, extensive application, and critical evaluation. This resource will help baseball players and coaches develop all the necessary aspects for mastering the fundamentals and progressing to the college, Olympic, or professional level. You will learn physical and mental skills and strategies for offensive and defensive play on and off the field as well as suggestions for conditioning in and out of season.

Whether you are a coach or player, use *The Baseball Handbook* to help you establish goals, plan practices, pick the right players for the right positions, review strategies, and add new dimensions to your game.

Acknowledgments

The recording of my thoughts on the fundamentals of baseball has been a lifelong project, but it became an exciting prospect when plans to write this book began to develop. I called upon my experiences as a student, athlete, coach, teacher, and athletic administrator to collect this material.

As I began writing, it became evident that a major portion of what I was writing was a collection of ideas and theories from men who taught me how to play and teach the game. I can honestly say that I have never watched, listened to, played for, or worked with a coach from whom I did not learn one idea. However, giving proper recognition to all those indispensable sources who contributed to my success today would be impossible. I will mention a few whose influence made my immediate success possible.

First of all, I was fortunate to play Little League Baseball for former Washington Senator Al Sparra and successful youth coach Bob Campbell. These men taught me to play a professional style of baseball that put me years ahead of my contemporaries. Later I played for and coached with the legendary Major League Baseball scout and amateur coach, Walter Youse. Without realizing it, he instilled in me the pride of being a champion. Youse, along with Jim Foit and George Henderson, stressed the "Oriole way," developed by Harry Dalton, Earl Weaver, George Bamberger, and Cal Ripken, Sr. They stressed organization, instruction, and achievement; the Oriole way is still one of the most popular and admired styles in baseball.

I'd like to acknowledge Dr. Marvin Eyler, who challenged his coaching students to be a teacher first and a coach second. This simple dare was my motivation as a lifetime learner of baseball. I am grateful to my players for their pride, desire, skill, and determination. I have had the opportunity to coach some of the best young baseball players in the United

States. Their accomplishments gave me the confidence to grow as a coach of elite athletes at the highest levels of amateur baseball.

Last but not least, I want to thank all my assistant coaches at the nine-time state champion Arundel High: Nick Jauschnegg, with the Mayo American Legion World Series Champions; Charles "Tut" O'Hara, with USA Baseball's junior national team; Rob Fornesier of Minnesota; George Sykes of Tennessee; Jim Fuller of Michigan; John Sawyer of Georgia; Mark Johnson of Colorado; and Ray Korn of New Jersey.

Key to Diagrams

B	batter
R	runner
CO	coach
P	pitcher
C	catcher
1B	first baseman
2B	second baseman
3B	third baseman
SS	shortstop
∿∿∿→	hit
– – – →	throw
⟶	run

1

Fundamentals Before the Fundamentals

Sport not only presents the opportunity to build character; it reveals character.

Your success as a player or coach will depend more on your rational investigation of the principles and concepts than any other single factor. This will be your personal philosophy, and will guide and direct you throughout your career.

Developing a Strong Philosophy

Team players and coaches must develop an athletic philosophy that will guide all they do on the baseball field. Choosing freely influences values, motivation, behavior, communication, discipline, rules, training methods, and ultimately character. Philosophies must be well defined. Most important, you as a coach must believe in your philosophy because it will reflect the way the game is coached, practiced, and played.

Attitude

One's attitude toward competition centers on three objectives of sport—fun, learning, and winning. To develop a philosophy, establish the three objectives in order of importance and communicate the ranking to all participants—coaches, players, umpires, and fans. There is no correct answer, so just be honest with yourself. The order will clarify your objectives and guide your day-to-day decisions.

In my program, I believe in the *fun-learn-win* philosophy. The order of these three words offers the best chance to win because it places the ballplayer first, ahead of winning. Most players and parents place fun as the number-one objective. Fun as an objective means focusing on satisfaction, developing a positive self-image, and committing to the job at hand. The best teams have fun in practice and during games. In doing so, good chemistry develops between coaches and players.

Observation

Careful observation and analysis will lead to a desire to change. Change is a bend in the road; it is not the end unless you fail to make a turn. Progress will not occur without change, but recognize that not all change is progress. With change come both rewards and failures. Be sure to stress rewards rather than punishments. Using this method can be difficult because it requires patience and proper planning. Planned rewards should recognize performance, effort, achieving intermittent steps toward goals, and the learning and performance of character. Offer reward when players earn it, rather than as the result of winning.

Failure is not fatal, but failure to change may be. Remember this: When you have finished changing, you're through. Baseball is a game of constant adjustment. Every time you fail to take advantage of something to make yourself better, you automatically become worse.

Development

Developing a strong philosophy essentially means developing strong players, first as individuals, then as a team. Placing the development of athletes above winning leads to long-term achievement. This development involves acquiring the motor skill needed to play baseball, knowing how and when to use the various strategies, knowing the rules and basic officiating, being physically prepared and psychologically ready for practices and games, playing fairly, and accepting responsibility.

One of the best ways to develop a well-rounded team is to visit other teams to observe their programs. Look for similarities, not differences. The idea is to enhance your philosophy, not to change it radically.

When watching other teams, always scout them because one of them may someday be an opponent. Also, look for fun and profit. Perhaps you can steal an idea to add to your program. This has all been made easier by baseball clinics, television, magazines, books, and videotapes.

Learning to Lead

The only way anyone can be his best is through learning. I have long believed that coaches and athletes must realize that the athletic field, court, or ball diamond is an extension of the classroom, a place where learning is much more than just preparing to win. Athletes must constantly learn about their sport, about their coaches and teammates, and most important about themselves.

Leading

Learning is not only about technique—about how to hit a grounder or make a double play—but about being able to guide others in the team philosophy. We look for sincere leadership. We often use small-group practices apart from the coach and 12-minute conditioning runs outside the view of the coach. We provide a variety of opportunities for leadership. During the game, starters and nonstarters alike must find their niche for leadership. Nonstarters coach first base; maintain charts; and steal signs from coaches, the catcher, or infielders. Because we consider this information important and necessary to the outcome of the game, we ask the ones who chart to communicate with their teammates. When we are successful, the coaches make a major issue of these roles.

Fair Play

Learning to compete honorably is a huge goal. It is a major priority, equal in importance to winning. Winning is not enough. We must win with class.

While winning, coaches, players, umpires, and spectators must constantly uphold the honor and dignity of the game. To do this, we attempt to follow the code of ethics of both the National Federation and USA Baseball. These codes emphasize the importance of high-level sportsmanship, ideal character, honesty, dignity, and high moral conduct. Specifically, they call for ethical game conduct such as a ban on bench jockeying; an active role in the prevention of drug and alcohol use; and the competency of coaches.

Testing is often used to improve coaching competency and learning efficiency. Those tests include an evaluation of baseball tools, skills, physical fitness, and game performance. Preliminary testing and the other principles of training determine readiness for participation. Then game results are used to evaluate coaching and instruction, learning by the ballplayers, and fairness of the competitive task. Simply, why did we win or lose? Chapter 4 presents some tests you can use to evaluate your coaches, players, and overall program.

Eleven Crucial Factors for Championship Baseball

1. Develop a **winning philosophy** centered on fun, learning, and winning. It is necessary to control the game of baseball on the field and the game of life off the field. Competition against better opponents will challenge your philosophy. The games your team plays against bigger, stronger, faster, and more skillful athletes will be intense. A winning philosophy is not a sometime thing. It is an eternal thing.

2. **Organization** is necessary in all phases of the game, both on and off the field. Organization is a way to differentiate luck from the permanence of ability.

3. **Discipline** is caring—wanting to do things right, wanting to learn, wanting to know more about what you are doing, wanting to look good and to give a good impression of yourself. It is the will to persevere and to sacrifice a few things, especially when people ask why. You must practice discipline until it is not discipline at all, but just what you do every day.

4. Surround yourself with **quality people** as assistant coaches, officials, players, and support personnel. Coachable players will win more often than gifted athletes with attitude problems. Delegate coaching responsibilities so that your assistant coaches prepare significant aspects of the program. Hire coaches who can teach and communicate. But remember that for some lessons experience is the only teacher. The best coach is one who has enough sense to pick good people to do what he wants done and enough self-restraint to keep from meddling with them while they are doing it.

5. **Style of play** creates an image. This image can affect opponents, umpires, and fans because it instills execution, consistency, and intensity in players. Winning is a habit. Unfortunately, so is losing. Therefore, as long as you are going to take the field, you must play to win.

6. Establish **realistic goals** that challenge the potential of each player and the team. Achieving these short-term and long-term goals requires athletic ability, talent, effort, desire, and determination. The most difficult goals are those most worthy of achievement. Consider the highest goal that you believe you can reach and then convince yourself that you can attain it. Confidence is everything.

7. **Unselfishness** means doing things to win games, not to achieve statistical goals. There is no limit to accomplishment if it doesn't matter who gets the credit.

8. **Communication** with players and coaches is necessary for basic understanding. Coaches, like players, have different personalities. The great ones excel at teaching, preparation, managing game situations, motivation, maximizing potential, and winning.

Understanding human behavior is crucial. If a player has a problem with academics, discipline, alcohol, drugs, or relationships, the coach must resolve it. The coach must not tolerate clubhouse lawyers (those who second-guess coaching decisions). They are the cancer of communication.

9. **Exploit mistakes** the opponent makes. The offense must be able to put the opponent under pressure and then take advantage of mistakes through aggressive and alert base running and hitting. The defense must also be able to execute plays and be ready to make opponents pay the price when they make a mistake. The team that strikes out the least, makes the fewest errors, gives up the fewest bases on balls, and hits the fewest fly balls, usually wins.

10. **Practice under pressure** so that you are prepared for pressure situations. As you probably know, it is much easier to play under pressure—when you need to come from behind or hold a lead to win—if practices have been as intense as games. Championship teams are well organized and have practiced under pressure in realistic, gamelike situations. Practice itself is not enough. It must be intelligent practice that is always working toward self-improvement.

11. Coaching **leadership** is necessary for success. Do you play aggressively and play to win? Or do you play it safe and play not to lose? Great teacher-coaches understand human behavior, establish goals that are demanding yet realistic, innovate, and take risks. The greatest mistake a coach can make is to be afraid to make one.

Pyramid of Achievement

For many years I admired the wisdom of the great basketball coach John Wooden of UCLA. His famous pyramid of success always made me think, but it never quite fit my beliefs. For the purposes of baseball and my own personal philosophies, I created a pyramid of achievement based on the pyramidial theories of Wooden and Maslow.

Like Wooden, I present a hierarchy of achievement in the form of a pyramid. The idea is that although success consists of a multiplicity of factors, some are more basic than others. Consequently, you can use a pyramid to rank the things athletes must have to thrive and succeed. The basic factors come first. You must meet those concepts before we can fully meet the other factors. The first level of emotional factors must be satisfied before next level can emerge. If the ballplayer is to reach competitive self-actualization, he must be emotionally stable (see figure on page 7). The factors are arranged in five levels, starting with the fundamentals at the base and progressing upward.

Level One

The foundation of the pyramid is the concept of *love* . . . loving the game. The constituent parts of the emotional levels are labor, understanding, respect, responsibility, and enthusiasm. This emotional foundation allows for solid construction of the pyramid.

Labor is the vivacity necessary to prepare for success willingly. Baseball players must be willing to work hard. The harder you work, the harder it is to surrender. Accomplishing tasks requires both effort and approach. It is important to learn efficiency. Success requires both hard work and efficient work.

Understanding is the harmony of good friendship. A baseball player must put himself in his teammates' shoes. Understanding occurs only if you put yourself in the other's place.

Respect is a loyalty, honesty, and truthfulness demonstrated by not exploiting teammates. Baseball players must not use each another. Basic honesty allows one to look in a mirror and be unashamed. If a positive team spirit is to develop, players must trust and know that all their teammates can do it right.

Responsibility is a voluntary commitment to a cooperative partnership with careful evaluation of the consequences. Baseball players must develop character to be recognized as blue-chip athletes. Character is the basic dependability of a player. Everyone wants people who can always be counted on.

Enthusiasm is the power, boldness, and eagerness of positive esteem. Baseball players must play and practice with enthusiasm to make the parts of loving the game effective. You have to show your love of the game. Win or lose, I want the fans to leave saying to themselves, "That team really loves to play."

Pyramid of achievement.

Level Two

The secondary level of the pyramid involves the mental aspect of the game—self-discipline, concentration, mental toughness, and determination.

Self-discipline is patience, tenacity, and control to set goals and satisfy the need for fun and worthiness. Baseball players must take control of their own practice, often by working out on their own. Look for people who come early and stay late.

Concentration means to focus intently with attention to detail. Baseball players must develop routines that trigger the ability to block out distractions, such as noise, nagging injuries, verbal abuse, and past failures. Seek players who can eliminate distractions and bear down.

Mental toughness means taking the lead without fear of failure or intimidation. Baseball players must learn from failure by analyzing and correcting.

Determination is the persistence of ambition and purpose necessary to accomplish goals. Players must put in time and effort to succeed at something. The desire for success and the willingness to work for it mark the difference between a championship team and a second-division team. Some ballplayers succeed because of natural, inherent talent, but many more succeed because of determination.

Level Three

Level three of the pyramid begins the physical development of the tools necessary to play baseball. These are conditioning, technique and tactics, and team spirit.

Conditioning is a state of mental, moral, and physical fitness necessary to compete. Baseball players must be well rounded, not just physically trained. Look for the complete player.

Technique and tactics are the motor skills necessary to participate and the knowledge of how to use them. Baseball players must use their tools in a professional style of play.

Team spirit is a solidity of intrinsic characteristics of backbone, heart, soul, and substance. Baseball players must play with unity. The secret of winning is working more as a team, less as an individual. As a coach I play not my nine best, but my best nine.

Level Four

The fourth level involves the concepts of a self-image that includes poise and confidence. The way a player thinks and feels about himself and his role on the team is a self-image. A positive self-image is the key that opens the door to excellence. Self-image affects the entire team personality from appearance to body language.

Poise is a balance of temperament with the ability to play in any situation. Baseball players must practice under pressure if they expect to play under pressure.

Players with *confidence* have faith in themselves and know that they are prepared. Confidence is built step by step. Coaches start with something that the player does well and then rewards him with praise.

Level Five

At the top of the pyramid is competitive self-actualization—the ultimate goal of baseball. Competitive self-actualization is "being all you can be." Before every game we say, "play your best and your best will be good enough." And we mean it.

Develop a strong philosophy for your team, both individually and as a group. Create a good repertoire between coaches and players. Teach the skills and the rules. And remember, have *fun* doing it!

Coach and Player Roles and Communication

Every game is a self-portrait of the person who coached it. Autograph your work with excellence of character.

The coach's job is to establish an environment that permits the assistants and players the opportunity to be the best they can be. You can create a solid working environment in a variety of ways.

1. **Give everyone responsibility.** Players need to feel that if they don't do the job it won't get done. They also need to know that when they accomplish something they will share in the accolades. Achievement is boundless when it doesn't matter who gets the credit; however, everyone deserves proper recognition.

2. **Let them know you care,** that you are interested in each individual, and that you are supportive and loyal. Carefully evaluate the consequences of your behavior before acting. Be certain not to exploit anyone. Put yourself in their shoes to enhance understanding. Demonstrate the commitment that you ask of others.

3. **Assist them in making good decisions.** Teach and guide them how to make the decisions that you want them to make. Never tell them what to do. Rather, encourage them to do what is best.

4. **Treat them as winners,** and they will win.

5. **Playing with good sportsmanship should be as important as playing to win.** There is no dishonor in playing with civility. Today's kids are concerned about rights and privilege, rather than responsibilities or obligations. Instill in your players the concept of fair play, and do it now. You can't build a reputation on what you are going to do.

6. **Motivate, reward, and emphasize.** Many coaches have solid knowledge of baseball and can effectively teach skills and strategies, but being a competent coach requires much more than that. Good coaches understand motivation. They know that intrinsic rewards are those that are internally satisfying to players. Good coaches have empathy. They not only understand but also feel the ballplayers' joy, frustration, anger, and anxiety. Demonstrate respect for your athletes by showing that you care.

7. **Avoid boring and repetitive practice sessions.** Baseball must excite and stimulate both players and coaches. It must be fun to play. Coaches should change practice regularly, be enthusiastic, encourage player input, and play baseball games during practice. Every player needs to have an important role on the team. Because only nine people play at a time, the subs need to feel that they have a critical role in the game. Nobody should just sit and watch. Players can chart pitching, defense, or offense or keep the official scorebook. Other players can use stopwatches to time opponents and teammates to evaluate performances objectively. The key to bench work is for the coach to demonstrate its importance to the team. Players must understand that bench work will help the ballclub win.

8. **Plan for success.** Good coaches are teachers first, coaches second. All coaches need to plan for the season. If there is not a plan for success,

there is still a plan . . . a plan for failure. Some coaches dislike the tedious part of the job. They prefer to recruit and compete.

9. **Allow adequate time for review.** After every practice and game, the coach must reevaluate the session concerning team goals and quality of performance. To facilitate this, the coach should take notes during the game or practice. I suggest that the scorekeeper (on the bench) jot notes on the scorebook during the game. In the postgame meeting, you and the team should review all points. It is important to be positive and not excessively critical. People will handle criticism best after a win, whereas after a loss the discussion will be difficult.

The entire coaching staff should evaluate themselves each year to identify strengths and weaknesses. The wise head coach will put his assistant coaches in positions of responsibility, where their coaching can produce significant results. Let your coaches coach! Then at season's end allow them to offer constructive criticism of the program. Your assistants should be active owners of the program rather than order-following lackeys. Permit the staff develop a plan to correct weaknesses, enhance strengths, and then do the necessary work to execute the plan.

10. **Communicate.** The importance of communication is so absolute that we devote an entire section to it.

Communication

Communication is the key to any coaching experience. If you can't tell your players what you want, how can you expect them to know what to do? Communication comes in many styles. Pick what works best for you, keeping in mind that the main objective is making sure that players understand you and that you understand them.

Coaching Style

Coaches use various styles, such as the command or dictator type, the buddy-buddy style, and the cooperative type.

Command-Style Coaching

Command-style coaching, also known as dictator or objective-competitor coaching, is a very popular method with inexperienced coaches having low self-esteem. These coaches often feel that they possess all the knowledge and experience and therefore, it is their right to make all the decisions. This kind of coaching style lacks confidence for the players to think for themselves. Without a doubt, this can be an effective style if winning is the major goal. However, the biggest danger in adopting this style is destroying the players' intrinsic motivation to simply play the game.

Buddy-Buddy Style Coaching

In buddy-buddy style coaching, the coach makes very few decisions, offers little instruction, provides little guidance, and solves few problems. The objective in this style is for the players to have a good time. This is the infamous "roll out the ball" type leadership. Because of his submissive behavior, these baseball clubs seldom win or achieve individual excellence. This style is the direct opposite of command-style coaching.

Cooperative Coaching

Cooperative coaching requires players and coaches to be responsible, with the coach retaining final responsibility. Players share involvement in the process. This modern interactive process demands both verbal and nonverbal communication. Coaches tune into the game of baseball and listen to their ballplayers. The objective of your coaching should be to make yourself obsolete. If you can get your ballclub on automatic pilot, you have accomplished the ultimate level of instruction. To reinforce the message, you must publicly announce your philosophy.

Verbal and Nonverbal Signals

Communication means not only sending messages but also receiving them. For example, listening and seeing may improve feedback. You must use your eyes and ears. Communicating nonverbally always involves a delivery with the proper emotion. To ensure credibility, verbal and nonverbal messages must agree. By following these nine rules to improve your communication skills, your team will know that you are sincere.

1. To establish credibility, always be consistent, fair, and reliable. Reward performance, not outcomes. Effort is what is most important. Be sure not to equate self-worth with winning.

2. In most cases, send positive messages but offer praise only when it is earned. Establish standards that your players can strive for.

3. Instruction must always be specific with good orientation. Reward players when they meet their goals, even the small ones.

4. Be a good listener. Whenever a player wishes to speak to a coach about a personal or team problem, the door should be open.

5. Develop excellent nonverbal skills. Players pick up many messages from the coach.

6. Use positive reinforcement to shape behavior and offer it frequently when players are learning new skills.

7. Teach baseball skills effectively by using sound pedagogy.

8. Reward important behaviors such as fair play, team play, and cooperativeness.

9. Use punishment sparingly. When you find punishment necessary, the punishment must fit the crime. Punish disruptive or dysfunctional behavior, not performance or effort. Many coaches have learned that punishment works, but only in the short term. Positive reinforcement not only works but also changes behavior 85 percent of the time. Conversely, punishment leads to a fear of failure, which restricts the spontaneity of great performance and self-actualization.

Communication is the key to making great ball clubs.

Characteristics of Effective Baseball Teams

Well-documented results of educational research cite 13 statistically significant characteristics of effective schools. That information can apply to a baseball program. At the conclusion of your athletic season, I suggest that you evaluate how your baseball program fares on each characteristic.

Give your program a letter grade of A to E, based on the standard educational grading system, on each characteristic of an effective baseball team. Perform this self-analysis independently, without the help of other staff members. Then, and only then, you may wish to share your opinion with your staff. You want them to consider the self-analysis a positive effort to locate strengths and improve on weaknesses. Head coaches should use whatever they learn to make positive adjustments in their programs.

- Student-athlete progress is effectively monitored.
- Coaches consistently support a student-athlete code of behavior.
- Learning is the chief priority.
- A variety of opportunities for leadership are available.
- Players and coaches expect that all students will learn.
- Evaluation data is issued to improve coaching and learning.
- The head coach is viewed as an expert instructional leader.
- Both coaches and players have high expectations.
- Rewards are stressed rather than punishment.
- Coaches visit other programs to observe exemplary programs.
- A pleasant, orderly atmosphere exists with coach-directed activities.
- Adequate time is provided for review and practice.
- The entire staff evaluates themselves annually to find strengths and weaknesses.

General Code of Conduct

Demand a commitment to excellence and achievement. Excellence involves discipline, integrity, respect, and attention to dress code and equipment. Remember to document the rules concerning dress code, game and practice rules, and personal appearance and share them with players and parents at the preseason meeting to avoid any later misconceptions.

Discipline

Discipline develops from fundamental training and instruction about fair play, pride in personal appearance, and performance.

One of my former players may have said it best when he lamented, "Before I tried out for the team, I was scared of the discipline. But I'm a

---

baseball player and I know discipline is caring. It's a habit of caring. It's wanting to do things right, wanting to learn, to know more about what you are doing, wanting to look good, and give a good impression of yourself. It is the will to keep it, and giving up a few things, especially when people say, 'Why?' . . . until finally it is not discipline at all. It is just what you do every day."

Discipline results from a combination of character education, the players' love of learning, compassionate chastising, and teaching players to eliminate adversity as a distraction. By providing a set of rules for behavior, a code of conduct at the ballpark, and rules for baseball dress, everyone can better focus on the goals of the game. The following system of rules and regulations has worked well for me.

Integrity

You won't get very far without integrity. Players, coaches, umpires, parents, and fans—everyone is scruntinized for possessing integrity in their personal lives and as a ball club.

1. Be honest. It is the only way.
2. Do not use profanity, gamble, steal, smoke, drink alcohol, use drugs, chew tobacco, or take steroids. Stay out of any establishment that serves alcoholic beverages and away from parties where drinking or drug use is occurring.
3. During the season, be careful of activities that may impair your performance, such as swimming or being too long in the sun.
4. Keep your gripes to umpires to a minimum and watch your language. You have a right to disagree, but you do not have a right to be disagreeable.
5. Yelling back at fans is not permitted.
6. If you are sick or injured, tell the coach!
7. Do not make unkind remarks back at fans.
8. You are what you eat, so don't eat junk foods. Fat is the enemy of speed.
9. Be on time! Don't be late to meetings, practice, buses, and so on.
10. After practice, the real practice of self-discipline begins.
11. Use the expression "sir" and "ma'am" to faculty members and staff. It sounds better than any other form of an address.
12. No roughhousing, especially in the hotel, locker room, school, bullpen, or dugout.
13. Do not steal from your education by cutting class or by not doing schoolwork.
14. Stand tall and look proud. You are a baseball player.

Goals of the Athletic Program

- To develop such attributes as skills, confidence, integrity, and teamwork in competitive sports
- To develop useful habits of physical fitness and conditioning
- To develop courage, self-control, and the ability to survive
- To gain individual skills for enjoyment of sports after graduation

---

Respect

Showing respect to yourself, your team, your parents, your coach(es), and the opposing team is a necessary part of being a first-class person and ball player.

1. When in public wear the complete uniform, including the hat. The shirt should be tucked into the pants and the stockings rolled so that the back shows three fingers' width of the stocking.
2. Do not eat during the game.
3. Pitchers must wear sweatshirts with sleeves below the elbow.
4. Don't throw helmets, bats, gloves, or any equipment.
5. Wear helmets in games and practices on deck, at bat, on bases, and in the bullpen.
6. Catchers wear full gear in the bullpen or at batting practice.
7. Catchers must wear a helmet and cup when warming up a pitcher anywhere on the field.
8. Shower daily.
9. Keep the clubhouse and dugout clean by putting trash in the trash can.
10. Put equipment in the proper place, (i.e. Keep the carpet clean).
11. Ask to borrow equipment; do not merely take it.
12. Don't wear spikes indoors.
13. Don't lie around in or outside the dugout or bullpen, and stay out of the bleachers.
14. On the bus, no horseplay is allowed. Don't throw anything out the window.

Proper Dress

Proper dress is important both on and off the field for any athlete, so keep a neat, clean-cut, and well-groomed appearance. Sideburns must be no longer than the bottom of the ear and kept well groomed. There will be no goatees, mustaches, or other facial hair. Hair must be neat and trimmed, with no hair over the ears and hair off the collar. Do not wear hats in school or wear hats backward. That style shows a lack of respect and indicates that you are headed in the wrong direction. Pitchers should wear lightweight jackets or sweaters to protect their arms.

Proper Equipment

Having proper equipment on hand is always a bonus.

1. Baseball shoes: two pair, old and new. Shoes should be the same for all players in the ball club. Metal cleats are recommended.
2. Two sleeved shirts for home games and two sleeved shirts for away games.
3. A warm baseball jacket.
4. Two gloves, old and new.
5. Sliding pads.
6. Cup and supporter, especially infielders, catchers, and pitchers.
7. Shower shoes.
8. Six pairs of sanitary socks.
9. Two pairs of batting gloves.
10. Two $2\frac{1}{2}$-pound weights or dumbbells.

The spirit of achievement lives in all effective baseball teams. When a player does his best, it will always be good enough. Remind your players that it's not always the best player who wins; it's the team that is willing to pay the price in advance. Motivation to win is purely and simply raw ambition, high standards, great expectations, and realistic goals. Every play is a self-portrait of the ballplayer who did it. He should autograph his performance with excellence.

3

Mental Preparation

*Champions are not those who never fail;
they just never quit.*

When challenged by competition, athletes can find enjoyment. Competition must occur within the parameters of the team's ability. Over the long term, the emotional thrill of honest competition is the ultimate source of worthiness. This positive attitude is the determining factor in the motivation of ballplayers.

Motivation

Intrinsic motivation begins with goal setting. Players need to have a clear purpose for practicing, playing, and achieving in athletics. They need to know where they are going and be able to identify the target when they reach it.

Success and motivation come from achieving goals. Goals are tools that keep the players' heads and hearts pointed in the right direction. When players work toward appropriate goals, they never have to worry about their feet going the wrong way. Goals are markers that gauge success. They can be either outcome or performance goals. Outcome goals are never within the control of the player and therefore must be treated as dreams rather than obtainable goals. Performance goals, however, are completely under control of the athlete and can therefore be reached. Performance goals emphasize effort over results. There is no fear of failure because self-worth is not equated with winning. Use these guidelines to set goals.

- Establish specific and measurable performance goals.
- Divide performance goals into long-term, intermediate, and short-term goals.
- Be able to evaluate play or practice and adjust the goals.
- Set goals that encompass all areas of player development including technique, strategy and tactics, fitness, and mental toughness.

What Moves a Champion?

- **Motivation:** The intrinsic motivation of living up to one's potential should be more important than achieving competence at particular parts of the game.
- **Leadership:** Direction is needed to overcome adversity.
- **Determination:** A blend of mental toughness and physical talent is necessary to hate losing.
- **Selflessness:** Teammates credit each other for their success. You don't see jealousy. Rather, you see love.
- **Composure:** The ballplayer who loses his head, who can't remain cool, is worse than no ballplayer at all.

- Develop some outcome goals.
- Demonstrate intrinsic motivation.
- Write plans to demonstrate a systemic approach to training as it relates to periodization concepts. This approach must account for practice time, rest, and competition.

Overcoming Adversity

Learning to overcome adversity will benefit the player both on and off the baseball diamond. We learn more from our failures than we do from our successes. A philosophically based plan can help the player deal with failure. Here is a partial list of guidelines:

1. The player must be willing to risk failure.
2. And yet he must passionately hate failure. He should think to himself, "I don't mind the bitterness of being beaten, but I deplore losers."
3. Persistence is critical, as is the willingness to acknowledge failure and go forward. The difference between an unsuccessful player and one who succeeds is not lack of strength or lack of knowledge but lack of will.
4. An honest self-evaluation of potential is how the player handles adversity.

Will to Win

The field may be merely the neighborhood sandlot. It's not the World Series or the NCAA championship, just bragging rights to determine the best in the neighborhood. It's an event unworthy of legendary prose. Nevertheless, it is the site where legendary heroics often begin. From such insignificant beginnings, players first begin to experience the excitement of victory and the pain of defeat. It is the insatiable need for victory that instills one's desire to be the best.

Dedication

Much more than the clichés about extra effort we read on the sports page, dedication is self-image, work ethic, and commitment never to give up. These are the characteristics of athletes who come early and stay late. Great athletes work hard off the field, independently developing the tools and perfecting the skills necessary to accomplishing their goals.

Though his chances of achieving fame and glory are slim, this athlete is not deterred. When he faces superior talent, he does not allow it to affect his style of play. He continues when others quit, creating a victory. Every victory is worth the effort . . . a satisfying reward for a job well done . . . a magnificent reward for his effort.

Determination

To be successful, players have to be willing to pay the price in advance. An entire set of strategies, tactics, and attitudes has defined championship baseball. Successful players use every conceivable method within the rules to win. They are imaginative, inventive, and have a solid foundation in fundamentals. By using speed, finesse, and tactics such as aggressive base running, professional-style hitting, outstanding pitching, a comprehensive defense, and most important, by using their heads, they win championships.

Great ballplayers show focus, determination, and mastery of the fundamentals of baseball.

Elite baseball players are perfectionists in the scientific style of play. Their unique style is often copied, but never mastered. Superior players are the masters that others pretend to be. Everything they do depends on their ability to play together in the professional style of inside baseball.

Concentration has been the name of the game, their key to success. They have the ability to block out distractions, using a two-part process of identifying a target for action and having a method to look at the target and take in all necessary information. Proper preparation increases the chances of responding quickly and properly. Teach your players the following keys to becoming a successful fundamental player.

1. Know the inning, the score, the number of counts on the hitter, and the position of base runners.
2. Know the offensive assignment for every situation.
3. Know the defensive assignment for every situation.
4. Anticipate active involvement in every play and react accordingly.
5. Check the field to determine whether it is fast or slow, whether the baseball carries or dies, and how the baseball bounces off the barriers and corners.
6. Always know the wind and sun conditions.
7. Think and plan for the opportunity to react to any situation or crisis.

Champions are not those who never fail; they just never quit. These ballplayers have no fear of failure. They see adversity as an opportunity to succeed. They visualize accomplishments, recognize sacrifice, know the ingredients, and are willing to preservere toward the goal.

4

Skills and Performance Evaluation

"The best coach is the one who has sense enough to pick good athletes to do what he wants done and enough self-control to keep from meddling while they do it."—the Daily Practice Plan

O ne of the most important decisions a ballplayer makes is selecting a position. If he makes a rational decision, the ballplayer can excel and be the best he can be. He can maximize his potential. Too often, however, ballplayers choose a position based not on tools but on one of numerous nebulous reasons.

Selecting Positions

Too often young players are forced to specialize on one defensive position to achieve the goal of winning. This indicates that coaches are imposing a professional model on these youths and focusing almost exclusively on winning. To win, these adult coaches believe that the best players must play all the time and in the most important positions.

You must decide what is most important. Is it winning? Or is it learning what it takes internally to win, that is, self-determination, concentration, hard work, and a passion for the game?

USA Baseball's Coaches' Education program recommends that players younger than 12 learn to play all nine positions with positive instruction in techniques and strategy, less emphasis on specialization, and an opportunity to develop leadership qualities. In that way kids will have more fun.

Skilled 12-year-olds and young teenagers should concentrate on five positions. The professional model is excellent for youths younger than 14 years old in determining which positions to learn at a higher level of competence.

Once high school begins, players should set their sights on two or three positions where they can get the maximum results from their tools and excel. That age is the time for a player to become a specialist.

Every position has unique requirements for competency. For position players, the five evaluation criteria are hitting, power, running, arm strength, and fielding. Each of these five fundamental baseball tools has a stereotypical degree of importance. The diagram on page 29 illustrates the various positions on the infield and outfield. For pitchers, the criteria are a fastball, curve, slider, any other pitch, control, mound presence, and aggressiveness (see table 4.1).

Baseball players are graded on a scale of two to eight, with five indicating average major-league ability. The sum of the grades is the professional baseball "overall future performance," or OFP. An OFP of 50 is viewed as the average for major-league baseball. Using this professional model, the player should select the position that offers the best chance for success. When evaluating the potential for a player, use two criteria, one for pitchers and the other for position players (see table 4.2, page 31 and the tools evaluation form on page 30).

This evaluation is used to project what level of baseball a player may achieve; therefore, aptitude, and the ability to make adjustments are more important than past or present performance.

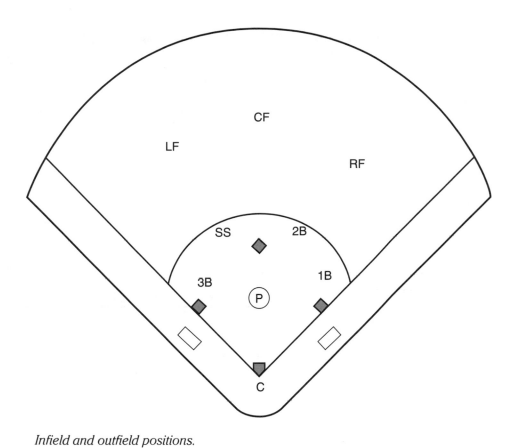

Infield and outfield positions.

Table 4.1	**Baseball Tools in Order of Importance**				
First baseman	Power	Hitting	Fielding	Arm	Speed
Second baseman	Fielding	Speed	Arm	Hitting	Power
Third baseman	Hitting	Power	Fielding	Arm	Speed
Shortstop	Fielding	Arm	Speed	Hitting	Power
Catcher	Fielding	Arm	Hitting	Power	Speed
Pitcher	Velocity	Movement	Breaking	Control	
Left fielder	Power	Hitter	Fielding	Arm	Speed
Center fielder	Fielding	Hitting	Speed	Arm	Power
Right fielder	Power	Arm	Fielding	Hitting	Speed
Designated hitter	Hitting	Power	Speed		
Courtesy runner	Speed	Stealing			

Professional Baseball Tools Evaluation

Bench press:_____   Lat Pull:_____   Jump-Reach:_____
Power Clean:_____   Squats:_____   Dead Lift:_____
60 Yard speed:_____   Trial#1:_____sec   Trial#2:_____sec   Trial#3:_____sec
Arm strength:_____   Trial#1:_____mph   Trial#2:_____mph   Trial#3:_____mph
Fielding:_____   Hitting:_____   Power:_____

Baseball Goal Setting

Goals: To be....._____
          To be....._____
          To be....._____

Deadline: _____
          _____
          _____

Ingredients: _____
          _____
          _____

Visualization: _____
          _____
          _____
          _____
          _____

"HUSTLE does not take any ABILITY!
It just takes **PRIDE & DESIRE!**
No excuses for not **HUSTLING!"**

"The best never rest."

"Victory happens when ten-thousand hours of training meet one
moment of **opportunity."**

Excellence is the result of **caring** more than others think is wise;
risking more than others think is safe. **Dreaming** more than others
think is practical and **expecting** more than others think is possible."

CREATORS
"For those empowered with the vision, greatness begins with a single
spark of inspiration."

Tools evaluation form.

Table 4.2	**Professional Baseball Grading System**						
	Radar	Time to 1B(R/L)	60 yards	Steal	Pitcher release	Catchers release	Raw power
8 Outstanding	94-96	4.0/3.9	6.4	3.00	0.8	1.6	420'
7 Very good	92-93	4.1/4.0	6.6	3.10	1.0	1.8	390'
6 Above average	89-91	4.2/4.1	6.8	3.15	1.2	1.9	375'
5 Average	85-88	4.3/4.2	7.0	3.25	1.3	2.0	360'
4 Below average	81-84	4.4/4.3	7.3	3.30	1.4	2.1	330'
3 Well below	76-80	4.5/4.4	7.5	3.40	1.6	2.3	300'
2 Poor	72-75	4.6/4.5	7.7	3.50	1.8	2.5	275'

The next suggested evaluation is a psychological evaluation of the player's baseball motivation. One method I have both developed and used successfully is to allow the player, and then a close teammate, to rate subjectively each of several motivational traits.

Next to each of the nine traits, I cite a famous player who I believe to be an excellent standard for comparison. Each of these major-league players is rated an eight because each possesses that particular trait in abundance. Therefore, ask each ballplayer to rate himself compared with these elite Major-League stars (see form on page 33).

Identifying Offensive Styles

The next step is to identify an offensive style. During player selection many ballclubs neglect to consider offensive styles. Coaches must consider not only defensive positions but also batting order.

Offensive philosophy and strategy will determine the characteristics desired for each place in the batting order. Placing players in the correct order will force the pitcher to give hitters good pitches to hit. We suggest the following ideas.

The leadoff hitter must have speed and hit with some power. A good eye and the personality not to worry about statistics are essential because he will be asked to set the table by taking the pitch on 1-0, 2-0, 3-1, and 3-0 counts.

The second batter must be an unselfish contact hitter with good speed. Hit-and-run skills are far more important than sacrifice-bunting skills because the sacrifice bunt is seldom used. A left-handed hitter is preferred because with a runner on first base the first baseman will play near the bag to hold him close.

First and second batters should be strong runners with good speed.

The third spot is usually occupied by the hitter with the highest batting average. The fourth batter, the cleanup hitter, should make good contact with good power. He needs the RBI mentality.

The fifth spot is the key position in the top of the order. He must be a tough out with the mental toughness to hit in the clutch. Obviously, home-run power and RBI numbers are desired.

The sixth hitter needs some power and must be a good RBI man.

The seventh and eighth hitters are often the weakest two in the lineup. Ideally, the eighth hitter will have characteristics similar to those of the second hitter, especially the ability to hit breaking balls. The last hitter should be similar to your leadoff hitter.

Testing Fitness

Fitness testing is the fourth tool used to evaluate personnel. Regardless of position, physical fitness, conditioning, and training are necessary in the pursuit of excellence. This testing should be done periodically, and

Baseball Questionnaire and Testing Form

Name:_____ Grade:_____ Age:_____ Position:_____
Address:_____ Ht.:_____ Wt.:_____ Bat:_____ Throw:_____
Community:_____ Zip:_____ Phone:_____ B-day:_____

What other positions do you have experience playing?_____
What is your greatest strength?_____
(Arm strength - running speed - fielding - hitting - power hitting)
What is your greatest weakness?
What other extra-curricular activities do you participate in?_____

Baseball History

	Team	Games played	Position	Batting Order
2001 Fall				
2001				
2000				
1999				
1998				

Sport Psychology

1. Aggressiveness: Jason Kendall   2 3 4 5 6 7 8   Hard worker, asserts himself
2. Ambition: Craig Biggio   2 3 4 5 6 7 8   Wants to be a winner
3. Coachability: Alex Rodriques   2 3 4 5 6 7 8   Willing to accept coaching
4. Consciousness: Denny Neagle   2 3 4 5 6 7 8   Does things as correctly as possible
5. Determination: Todd Helton   2 3 4 5 6 7 8   Sticks with it
6. Emotionality: Mike Mussina   2 3 4 5 6 7 8   Can handle his feelings well
7. Leadership: Dave Johnson   2 3 4 5 6 7 8   Wants to be in charge of others
8. Mental toughness: Paul O'Neil   2 3 4 5 6 7 8   Can take chewing out
9. Responsibility: Raphael Palmerio   2 3 4 5 6 7 8   Accepts responsibility and fame
10. Self-confidence: Barry Bonds   2 3 4 5 6 7 8   Sure of himself and his abilty
11. Trust: Cal Ripken, Jr.   2 3 4 5 6 7 8   Accepts people at face value

"Winning is a result of character."

records should be kept to evaluate long-term progress and areas where players need to improve.

Fitness testing should be conducted regularly several times a year. The purpose is to measure and evaluate a player's fitness and assess the need to develop strength, speed, and aerobic fitness.

Any standardized fitness test will work. The test should include the following items: vertical jump, upper-body strength (pull-ups), abdominal strength (curl-ups), agility (shuttle runs), speed (60-yard dash), aerobic fitness (mile run), arm strength (radar gun), and lean-body measurement (skinfold test). Records must be kept for comparative purposes. See chapter 5 for more details on fitness, diet, and conditioning.

The evaluation process is crucial to achieving both individual and team goals. The objective of evaluation is to put players in positions where they can excel. The wrong position may lead to poor performance and failure to reach maximum potential (self-actualization).

If players are put in their best position and in the proper spot in the batting order, they have a chance to excel and so does the team.

5

Physical Conditioning

I never said it would be easy;
I just said it would be worth it.

A baseball physical-conditioning program must develop explosiveness. This can be accomplished with speed-strength training, both in season and off. The program should include weight training, running, plyometrics, position-specific exercises, and diet.

Weight Training

The goal of sport-specific strength training is to concentrate on strength building and then, after several weeks or months, switch to lower weights and faster movements. In the off-season, players first need to establish a base of strength. After beginning to plateau, they should begin speed training and simply maintain existing strength.

After determining the goal the player must determine the number of days per week to work out. Three days per week is most common (e.g., Monday, Wednesday, Friday). Players should follow these simple rules in exercising the various muscles groups:

1. Exercise larger muscle groups first.
2. Alternate pull exercises with push exercises.
3. Alternate upper-body exercises with lower-body exercises.

The next step is to select the exercises to include in the basic strength-training routine. The players should select one or two per body area. The average routine includes approximately 12 exercises. Most of these are paired antagonistic movements, or push-pull exercises. Some effective exercises include the following:

Squat lift	Leg curls
Abdominal crunch	Leg extension
Dead lift	Bench press
Incline press	Seated rowing
Pull downs	Biceps flexion
Power cleans	Triceps extension

For all baseball players I recommend a combination of aerobic and anaerobic exercises. Pitchers should consider the daily running program described later in this chapter. Position players should consider an alternate-day (Tuesday, Thursday, and Saturday) program to develop power for hitting, general conditioning, and sprinting to develop running speed. This is also described later in this chapter. During the off-season, pitchers should have a daily throwing regimen with weight training three days a week (Monday, Wednesday, and Friday) and daily aerobic running. For position players, we suggest throwing three days a week (Monday, Wednesday, and Friday), conditioning and power-hitting training three days a week (Tuesday, Thursday, and Saturday), and then weight training.

Anaerobic weight-training exercises must include the power clean, dead lift, and squat lift. Players perform three to five sets of 6 to 12 repetitions at 70 to 100 percent of one maximal lift. The rest interval should be 90 to 150 seconds or until the athlete cannot complete another rep with full range of motion and controlled form.

Follow these general guidelines when designing a basic strength-training routine: Keep accurate records; change the routine approximately every four weeks; modify the routines to meet individual needs because no two individuals react the same to a given routine. Finally, realize that there is no secret routine. The secret to success is hard work!

POWER CLEANS

DEAD LIFT

SQUAT LIFT

ABDOMINAL CRUNCH

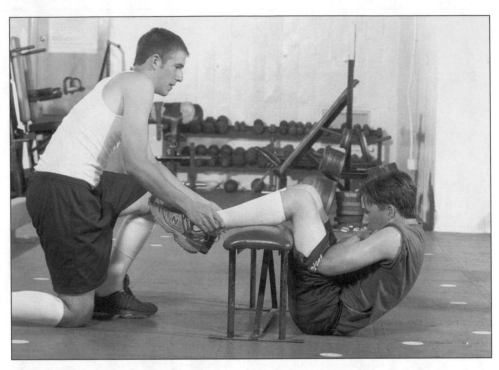

INCLINE PRESS

PULL-DOWN

LEG CURLS

LEG EXTENSION

BENCH PRESS

SEATED ROW

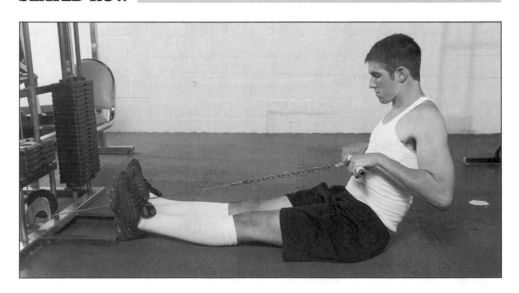

BICEPS FLEXION

TRICEPS EXTENSION

Hitters

Biomechanical analysis shows that about 50 percent of the force generated in batting and pitching comes from the trunk and shoulder girdle. Thus specialized exercises that train the rotational muscles are particularly beneficial. These exercises include: sit-ups with a twist, hyperextension back raises, and reverse trunk twists.

To enhance explosiveness when working out with medicine balls, players should use a variety of two-handed throws. If the balls are too heavy, form and technique will be compromised. Players should try to be fast and powerful rather than slow and strong.

SIT-UPS WITH A TWIST

HYPEREXTENSION BACK RAISE

REVERSE TRUNK TWIST

All baseball players benefit from a combination of aerobic and anaerobic exercise.

Position Players

To improve the ability to start and turn quickly, baseball players should perform a variety of lower-body exercises. These include single leg raises (which strengthen the leg muscles), plyometric lateral jumps over a bench (which enhances explosiveness), and Russian twists (horizontal shoulder rotations). The plyometric jumps will be discussed in more detail in chapter 6.

SINGLE LEG RAISE

To develop muscular explosiveness, players can also use a variety of jumps. We suggest the following depth jumps to develop lower-body explosiveness:

1. Step off a box, drop down, and then jump up and over six medicine balls, one by one, laid out in a row.
2. Climb a flight of stairs by doing forward or side jumps, taking two or three stairs at a time and moving as fast as possible.
3. Using any plyometric box, perform a jump pattern that includes all the sides of the box.

Several depth jumps can help develop arm explosiveness:

1. Push-up depth jumps. From the push-up position, leap off the floor and return to the push-up position.
2. Wheelbarrow hops. With a partner holding your legs, hop off the floor with small takeoffs.
3. Clapping hands push-ups.

Pitchers

The object of conditioning, warm-ups, and good body mechanics is to allow the player to operate at a level slightly below that which would cause him injury but still permit him to generate enough energy to defeat a player of equal ability. Being in good condition is more important for the pitcher than it is for anyone else on the team. To accomplish this goal by the first day of tryouts, pitchers must work on baseball-specific training at least six weeks earlier.

Warm-Up

The player should begin the workout with a three-minute cardiovascular exercise, such as a quarter-mile jog. He should include upper-body movements, such as arm circles, both single and double, in either direction. Because it is dangerous to stretch cool muscles, players should raise their body temperature before beginning this program.

The workout continues with static daily stretching for about six minutes. Using the 13 static stretches (known as TERPs) reduces the chance of injury and increases flexibility.

Next, pitchers play soft toss for 15 minutes, starting at a distance of 45 feet and working up to 200 feet. As the toss lengthens it is especially important to throw the ball low and hard and to avoid lobbing the baseball. The final 15 throws should be at 120 feet apart. Players should finish the workout by placing a hat on the ground about 15 feet in front of the partner as a target to reinforce proper mechanics at the release point.

Weekly Throwing Program

This weekly throwing program can be used in the preseason or off-season with little modification. But in-season throwing will require more rest in addition to daily throwing.

Heavy-Baseball Training (Monday-Wednesday-Friday)

This program is designed to develop arm strength! To accomplish this, pitchers must throw hard while focusing on arm speed with good mechanics; however, they need not worry too much about control.

It is best to work in pairs so that the pitchers can easily simulate the pitching of innings. We recommend that they throw about 16 pitches, but each inning should end with tolerance to prevent muscle injuries. During the first three weeks, pitchers should not exceed 50 pitches daily. Also, pitchers should never exceed 180 pitches with the weighted baseball in a week. If the heavy-baseball training is executed outdoors, it is especially important to keep the baseball dry.

Regimen

One set of 8 pitches	5-ounce baseballs
Rest	
One set of 16 pitches	6-ounce baseballs
Rest	
One set of 16 pitches	6-ounce baseballs
Rest	
One set of 16 pitches	6-ounce baseballs
Rest	
One set of 8 pitches	5-ounce baseballs

Batting-Practice Pitching (Tuesday-Thursday)

Pitchers throw to a catcher on flat ground in sets of about 15 pitches to stimulate an inning pitched. This is a great time for structured sequence throwing. For example, these throws may be in the pattern of fastball, slider, curve, and change-up.

Pitchers should be able to throw 20 minutes of batting practice after five days and in games after nine days. If the pitcher began the program at least six weeks before the first day of practice, he would be at nearly 100 percent.

Pitchers should not throw hard. They should work on technique from both the windup and set positions. This is the time to focus on pitching mechanics and concentrate on all pitches, including the change-up.

Cross-Training (Saturday-Sunday)

On the weekends pitchers should do some form of cross-training, perhaps by throwing a football to develop arm strength and throwing mechanics. When cross-training, they should work out to tolerance and be careful not to overexercise. A little cross-training can be fun!

In-Season Throwing

During the season, we prefer to use a five-day plan for the pitchers (see table 5.1). We believe this allows for adequate rest and recovery between assignments. Overuse is believed to be a major cause of arm injuries.

Relief Pitching

If a pitcher is to be used in relief, you must be extremely careful about the overuse syndrome. This aspect of coaching is truly an art, not a science. Most amateur teams do not have special relief pitchers, so the task of relieving falls on the regular pitchers. If a starter is used for a brief relief appearance, it should be the day after he has pitched several innings. He should never pitch in relief with only one day of rest. In either

Table 5.1	After Game Day Pitching Relief Schedule
Day 1	Warm up, soft toss for about 5 minutes, stretching, weight training, and distance running.
Day 2	Warm up, throw 20 pitches in the bull pen and use all pitches, stretching, weight training, and distance running.
Day 3	Warm up, pitch 10 minutes of hard batting practice, stretching, weight training, distance running.
Day 4	Warm up, very light throwing in the bull pen with the emphasis on mechanics and control, stretching, weight training, and distance running.
Day 5	Pitch in the game with limitations. When finished pitching, be sure to ice both the arm and shoulder.

case, he would then resume the regular five-day rotation described in table 5.1.

Distance Running

Some pitchers are only as strong as their legs; therefore, daily distance running is necessary. Strikeout pitchers, especially, must do a lot of running because striking out hitters requires pitch movement, a variety of pitches, and energy. Pitchers should plan to run every day for 25 to 45 minutes.

Pitchers should begin running at a slow pace for about two minutes, then run for one to two minutes at a fast pace. They repeat this cycle of slow interval running followed by fast intervals of speed for 25 to 45 minutes or until tolerance occurs. When running these bursts of speed, they must concentrate on proper running form, lifting the knees high and liberally flexing the arms without moving the head.

Shoulder Safety Exercises for the Rotator Cuff

The best way for a pitcher to prevent overuse injury to the shoulder is to maintain a good strengthening and flexibility program. The rotator-cuff tendons often become injured. We recommend daily work to prevent injury and help in rehabilitation to reduce soreness and pain. Stiffness and soreness on the front side are the result of poor mechanics, whereas stiffness on the backside of the elbow and shoulder are caused by lack of strength. The elastic-cord work should always precede a light dumbbell workout.

Although it may not seem to take enormous strength to throw a baseball, condition and endurance are still necessary ingredients in the pursuit of excellence. The rotator cuff in the shoulder must be strengthened and stabilized separately from the other shoulder muscles; therefore, typical upper-body free-weight exercises are not sufficient. The key to preventing shoulder injuries is to understand the anatomy of the shoulder complex and how other muscles affect throwing.

The shoulder consists of at least four major joints, more than 20 different muscles, and three very important bones. During the throw, a ballplayer accelerates the arm to speeds greater than 90 miles an hour, generating this speed from the legs, pelvis, trunk, shoulder, and arm. Typically, we expect the rotator cuff to slow down this process, after the throw. A ballplayer uses the largest muscles of the body to accelerate the arm and then forces four small muscles of the rotator cuff to stop the motion. Not only does this sound unfair, it cannot be done without injury.

It seems that the best way to prevent shoulder injury is to strengthen the muscles of the legs, pelvis, and trunk. Essentially, one can train shoulders for throwing by training the pelvis and trunk to slow down the forces they created.

For rotator-cuff weight training, pitchers should use three- to seven-pound dumbbells, performing seven sets of 15 to simulate seven innings of pitching. The TERPs exercises are a series of rotator-cuff actions used in a continuous motion—the idea is not to stop between each step.

TERPS

Six-count exercises done in seven sets of 15 to 20 reps

1. Supraspinatus shoulder abduction with thumbs down at 45 degrees to the body and return to the starting position.

2. Shoulder abduction to adduction over the head and return to the starting position.

3. Shoulder flexion with palms down.

4. With shoulders fully flexed, rotation to the palms-up position.

5. Elbow flexion while maintaining the high-elbow position.

6. Extension to the starting position.

TABLE EXERCISES

Seven sets of 15 to 20 reps

1. External rotation while lying on the side

2. Prone horizontal abduction

3. Behind-the-back towel stretching, alternating flexion and extension

LEG EXERCISES

Seven sets of 15 to 20 reps

1. Single left-leg deep squats with an elevated right leg on a bench

2. Balance-beam walk

FOREARM, ELBOW, AND WRIST EXERCISES

Seven sets of 15 to 20 reps

1. Forearm supination while seated. To do the pronation exercise, reverse the wrist movement, starting from a palm down and turning it upwards.

2. Wrist flexion while seated

3. Wrist extension while seated

4. Ulnar deviation

COMPREHENSIVE CONDITIONING EXERCISES

1. Carioca drills: three sets of 25-yard sprints in each direction
2. Standing sit-ups with elastic tubing for two sets to fatigue
3. Two-handed medicine-ball trunk throws for two sets to fatigue
4. Partner two-handed push-pulls for one set to fatigue

Running Program

Simply put, speed wins. Players on a quest to be the best must continually improve foot speed.

Conditioning Cues

Baseball personnel need simple methods to communicate without being too technical. We have learned that visual teaching cues offer an effective way to teach skills. Teaching cues are simple, straightforward instructional tools. Good visual cues help baseball players create visual images for better concentration. Table 5.2 on page 66 illustrates visual cues you can use to improve players' technique.

Dos and Don'ts

Do
- Lift your knees high. Reach out with your foreleg.
- Stay high on your toes.
- Reaching out, slap your lead leg to the ground.
- Swing your arms parallel to the direction of the run.
- Swing your arms from your shoulder.
- Bound forward, not upward.
- Maintain good forward lean.
- Keep your hips forward and back straight.
- Point your toes parallel to the run.
- Turn your head in the direction you wish to run.

Don't
- Grit your teeth or jaw.
- Look back.
- Run with your head down.
- Run all over the place. Do run in a straight line.
- Swing your head.
- Clinch your fists or extend your neck.
- Swing your arms across your chest or up in your face.
- Use a high rear kick.

Table 5.2	Teaching Cues for Short Distance*		
	Visual Cues	**Alternate Cues**	**Common Errors**
Hip-torso action	· Tall · Flat tummy · Buttocks tucked under	· Like being picked up by your hair · Make a pillar with hips and torso	· Too much forward lean
Arm action	· Hammer nails in the wall behind you	· Pump arms · Hands to shoulder · Thumb in pocket	· Arms crossing the midline of the body
Hand action	· Hold a newspaper	· Thumb on index finger	· Fists clenched · Floppy hands
Leg action	· Heel to buttocks · Step over opposite knee · Toe to knee · Snap leg down · Ground contact with ball of foot	· Kick buttocks · Thighs parallel to ground · Point toes to sky · Extend/reverse lower leg	· Not enough knee flexion · The knee lift too low, thereby, pointing the toe to ground before contact · Not snapping leg down · Stopping the foot on contact with the ground

*For distances of 90 feet to 20 yards.

Improving Speed

Improving speed is an important objective of any athletic conditioning program. More speed can result in better defensive performance, better baserunning, and better offensive results. Speed is often the first tool evaluated by a baseball scout; therefore, better speed is a valuable asset in career development.

Downhill Running

By using downhill running, players can increase running speed in two ways. One way is to increase the stride frequency, that is, the number of times the feet hit the ground. The second is to increase the length of the stride.

You must first locate a hill with a grade of less than 30 degrees that has a smooth, even straightaway marked off to provide a set distance for timed running. Use a stopwatch after the dry run and have players run in pairs. In this way you will introduce a little competition into the training and give players a sense of accomplishment as they gradually improve their times.

When running downhill, players will have the natural tendency to lean back, shorten their stride, and land flatfooted to overcome the force of gravity. They should concentrate, however, on using the same running techniques they use on a level straightaway. The force of gravity will naturally encourage them to increase stride frequency. This, combined with proper running form, should produce faster times.

Because races and games are rarely held on hills, we recommend that players also work out on a level straightaway for timed 40-yard sprints. The time on the downhill run will average about 0.2 to 0.4 seconds faster than the time on the level sprint.

Running Drills

Form Running at a Slow Pace

Purpose: To develop proper sprinting technique

Implementation:
1. Measure a distance of 60 to 100 yards from an outfield foul line.
2. Line up the entire squad on either outfield foul line.
3. Players run at about half speed for a distance of 60 to 100 yards, maintaining proper technique for the entire distance.

Jogging to Accelerations

Purpose: To develop proper sprinting techniques and speed

Implementation:
1. Measure a distance of 60 to 100 yards from an outfield foul line.
2. Line up the entire squad on either outfield foul line.
3. Players run for about half of the distance at half speed. At that point the coach blows a whistle. On the sound the runners vigorously pump their arms to accelerate to full speed to the finish.

Get-Ups

Purpose: To use competition to improve the start of a sprint

Implementation:

1. Have the team pair off so that each player has a partner, creating two groups. One group will be the chasers, and the other will be the prey. It is best if partners are of similar speed.
2. The prey sit on the foul line with feet and hands on the ground. Have the chasers stand five yards away in foul territory, aligned with their partners.
3. On the coach's command, the prey quickly get up and run for 90 feet while the chasers attempt to catch and tag their partners before they reach 90 feet.
4. After the sprint, have everyone walk back to the foul line. The paired runners then change roles, prey becoming chasers and chasers becoming prey.
5. Repeat the competition only three times.

Standing Triple Jumps for Distance

Purpose: To improve leg power and speed

Implementation:

1. Have players line up facing second base on the dirt part of the in-field foul line. This usually creates about five rows of players with several players in each row.
2. Players stand with the feet about shoulder-width apart with knees bent so that they are in an athletic position. They jump forward, landing on one foot, take a long step with the opposite foot, and then jump from that foot to a landing on both feet. The triple jump is also called the hop, step, and jump.
3. On the coach's command, each player will execute the triple jump for distance.
4. We recommend doing one set of 10 triple jumps, once a week.

Nutrition

Nutrition can affect performance in a variety of ways. Each day the body needs more than 50 nutrients. Over time, omission of any of these can harm health and hinder performance. Using good nutritional habits will not work overnight miracles, such as shaving half a second off a 60-yard dash time, but proper nutrition throughout the year can make a difference. By staying healthy and decreasing down time, players will feel better, train harder, and be in better condition, which could mean the difference between winning and losing.

Diet

A single perfect diet doesn't exist. Each ballplayer is different and has individualized needs. A 150-pound shortstop, for example, should eat differently than a 220-pound first baseman. The best diet is one that keeps the player well hydrated, provides adequate calories, and supplies the 50-plus nutrients in the needed amounts. No single food or supplement can do this. Adequate nutrition is best achieved by consuming a wide variety of foods each day.

We encourage baseball players to eat six small to three normal well-balanced meals daily, selecting foods from the various food groups. An adequate diet must supply the fuel necessary for performance. This diet is to the athlete what gasoline is to the automobile.

Contrary to popular belief, ballplayers do not need vitamin, mineral, protein, or carbohydrate supplements. By eating a balanced diet, an athlete can meet all nutritional needs.

To prevent stomachaches during competition, ballplayers should eat at least three to four hours before the game. They should eat a meal of easily digestible high-carbohydrate foods, consisting of choices of pasta, breads, low-fiber cereal, fruit juice, unfried potatoes, and bananas.

Players should avoid foods high in fat such as french fries, potato chips, and peanut butter. They should also try to avoid foods that are high in bulk such as beans, cabbage, lettuce, nuts, and spinach; and foods high in sugar such as cakes, candy, doughnuts, and honey. Energy for physical activity comes from the food eaten over the previous several days, not the food eaten an hour or so before a practice or game. There is no such thing as quick energy food or drink!

Vitamin pills do not give quick or extra energy because vitamins do not supply calories. Although B vitamins do help release energy from carbohydrates, fats, and protein, athletes normally get sufficient vitamins from their daily diet. Bee pollen, wheat germ, and other products advertised as energy aids do not work either.

Coffee, colas, and tea contain the stimulant drug caffeine and do not improve performance. Proper warm-up works much better. Caffeine causes headaches, stomachaches, nervousness, irritability, and diarrhea. Also, caffeine is a diuretic, or urine-producing drug, with the effect of increasing dehydration.

Water

The most important nutrient is the one most overlooked—water! Water is crucial because the human body is 60 to 70 percent water. A person can go weeks and even months without certain vitamins or minerals before noticing an effect, but without adequate water, performance can be affected in less than an hour. Water is necessary for the body's cooling system. It transports nutrients throughout tissues and maintains adequate blood volume. Dehydration can cause the body to overheat. Small unreplaced fluid losses can impair performance, and large unreplaced losses can cause heatstroke or even death.

If a player waits until he is thirsty to drink, he has waited too long. During intense exercise the body's thirst mechanism lags behind need. Players must make a conscious effort to drink water before they ever become thirsty. Actual requirement will vary depending on temperature and humidity, the intensity of the workout or game, and how well acclimated the player is. The most reliable indicator of how much water one needs is weight. In hot and humid weather, ballplayers can sweat off six pounds in an hour. Each pound of weight lost as sweat is equal to two cups of water. A person does not lose much fat in a short time. Therefore, players can obtain an accurate read on how much fluid they need to replace by weighing themselves nude, or in minimal clothing, before and after exercising. For each pound he loses, the player has a deficit of two cups of fluid that he should have drunk before and during the practice or game. All ballplayers should drink water before, during, and after practices and games.

The air in an airplane's passenger compartment is dry, so the body can lose a lot of fluid by evaporation while flying. For that reason, athletes should drink plenty of water before, during, and after air travel. The longer the flight, the more water one should drink. Alcohol and caffeine-containing beverages (such as coffee or cola) should be avoided because they increase water loss.

Sport drinks are fine to use as a fluid replacement after training or competition is over; however, caution should be used if they are consumed immediately before or during a competition. Sport drinks contain sugar and electrolytes. Sugar consumed during the 90 minutes before an endurance event (longer than 90 minutes of continuous effort) can increase the rate at which the body uses glycogen. After the first 30 minutes of an endurance activity, however, consuming a weak sugar solution may prevent low blood sugar and help performance. Water is probably the best replacement fluid for most ballplayers, although endurance athletes may benefit from the sugar content of sport drinks.

Replacement of electrolytes is important because they are involved in fluid balance, nerve conduction, and muscle contraction. But players need not worry about replacement until after exercise is over. Sweat contains small amounts of electrolytes and is actually less concentrated with electrolytes than other body fluids. When one sweats, the body loses much more water than it does electrolytes. During exercise, water replacement is the main concern. After exercise, players can easily replace electrolytes with a normal diet. Getting enough sodium is not a problem for most ballplayers. At most, it only takes a few extra shakes from the saltshaker. Potassium replacement may be a problem if the player doesn't eat fruits and vegetables. Citrus fruits and juices made from oranges, grapefruits, and bananas are excellent sources of potassium as are potatoes, tomatoes, and milk.

Vitamins and Minerals

Several of the B vitamins are involved in the process of converting fat to energy, but amounts above what one needs will not speed up this process. Taking large doses of vitamins is similar to trying to make a car run faster by putting seven spark plugs under the hood of a six-cylinder car. Intakes above the recommended dietary allowances (RDA) are not necessary and in fact can be toxic for some vitamins. Toxicity and other harmful side effects of large amounts of several vitamins and minerals are well documented. For example, the RDA for vitamin A is 1,000 retinol equivalencies (RE) for men and 800 (RE) for women. Toxic reactions can occur with as little as five times these levels, amounts not uncommon in many over-the-counter supplements. Overdoses of niacin, vitamin B6, vitamin C, vitamin D, iron, magnesium, zinc, and other have also been shown to be harmful.

Protein

Between 1.0 and 1.5 grams of protein per kilogram of body weight will be sufficient if calorie intake is high enough. For a 150-pound (68 kilogram) athlete, that need is 68 to 102 grams of protein. Approximately 10 grams of protein are contained in one once of meat, one egg, one glass of milk, one ounce of cheese, or four slices of bread. Studies have found that most athletes eat far more protein than they need. A more common problem for players on a heavy training program is that they don't eat enough carbohydrate calories. If the body doesn't have enough carbohydrate to use for energy, then it uses protein, which means that the protein isn't available to maintain muscle mass. Protein supplements offer no advantage over protein available from foods such as meat, milk, cheese, and eggs. In fact, research has shown that the protein quality of many so-called high-protein supplements is highly variable and often inferior to milk and egg protein. Note the difference between a normal teenage diet and a high performance diet used by athletes.

If a player is lifting weights to build muscles, he will need a little more protein than if he weren't lifting. But that doesn't mean he will need more than he is already eating. One pound of muscle is approximately 70 to 75 percent water, 15 to 20 percent protein, and 5 to 7 percent other material, such as fat, glycogen, minerals, and enzymes. So one pound of muscle contains approximately 70 to 105 grams of protein. If a player could put on one pound of pure muscle in two weeks, he would need 5 to 8 additional grams of protein each day. One additional ounce of meat or cheese a day or an extra glass of milk would be more than enough.

The body cannot store extra protein; it must either use it or lose it. If a person eats more protein than the body can use, the protein is broken down and part of it is either used for energy or stored as body fat. The other part, the nitrogen part, can be toxic in excess amounts. Large amounts of protein can lead to dehydration, stress the kidneys and liver, increase the amount of calcium lost in urine, and cause goutlike symptoms in joints.

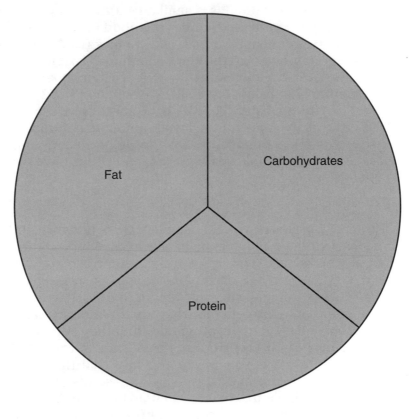

Normal teenage diet.

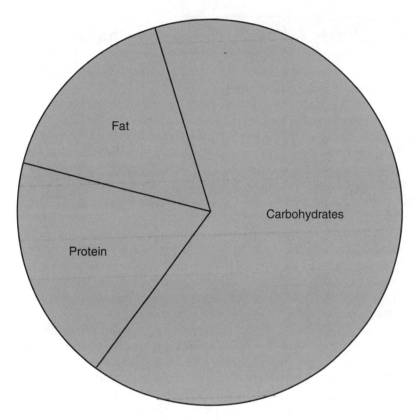

High-performance diet.

Amino acids are the individual units of protein, much like the individual links of a chain-link fence. They have become popular among strength-training athletes and are often taken because the athlete has been told they will stimulate an anabolic effect, increase the rate of muscle gain, or cause weight loss. They can be taken individually or in various combinations. One example is a combination of arginine and ornithine that is sold as a natural steroid. Another formula containing arginine and lysine is sold to cause weight loss. Arginine and lysine are amino acids found in foods. Ornithine is formed in the body as arginine is metabolized. The body cannot tell the difference between amino acids in pills or powders and the amino acids in foods. All are metabolized the same.

Conditioning is a life-long process that involves various periods during the year with specific objectives in each period. A well-planned conditioning program will result in overall better fitness for life, enhanced performance on the diamond, greater self-esteem and self-discipline, and better social relationships. To reap the benefits of training, you must plan and consistently follow a solid program. I never said it would be easy; I just said it would be worth it.

Fit or Fat by Choice or by Chance?

Bigger, stronger, faster are buzzwords for athletes. But if the goal is not properly planned, the result may be fatter, weaker, slower.

The fitter you are, the longer you live and the better you compete. Without doubt fat is the enemy of speed. That's why it has been observed that people with a body-fat percentage above 25 float easily and run slower.

The main function of fat is to provide energy for muscle. In the performance of all sports, however, fat people have a significantly higher percentage of inactive time than fit people. They simply move less and burn less energy.

Most overweight people eat less than underweight people do, yet they still become fatter, slower, and less active. Fasting encourages the body to become fatter, not leaner, because the internal chemistry of overweight people has adapted to a low-calorie intake. Subcutaneous fat must be thought of as belonging to the whole body.

Fatness is a vicious cycle. The more fat you have, the more your body chemistry, or metabolism, changes to favor the buildup of even more fat. We start to gain weight only when we have so excessively overeaten and underexercised that we exceed the capacity of the muscles to hold internal fat.

Exercise increases metabolic rate, increases the amount of muscle, raises the calorie-consuming enzymes inside the muscle, and increases the burning of fat. When fit people exercise, the pH of their blood changes, causing hunger to decrease. These changes force the body to use more fat as an energy source.

Exercise resets all body mechanisms to reduce body fat. Exercise influences the ultimate control mechanism, known as the set point. The set point is affected by heat production, muscle mass, blood sugar and insulin, hunger control, mood, and fat-cell enzymes.

The critical problem of fitness is not excess fat; it is the lack of athletically trained muscle. To correct this, we should exercise more often. Remember, if we're in a hurry to get in shape, we should exercise longer, not harder. We can train our muscles, increase our energy, and decrease our fat by following these guidelines.

- Exercise aerobically for time, not distance. Aerobic exercise using oxygen is the most efficient way to remove marbling fat. If you stay in the training zone, at 65 to 80 percent of maximum pulse rate, it takes just 20 minutes a day.
- Practice interval training such as wind sprints.
- Warm up first, stretch, and then work out.
- For motivational purposes, repeat to yourself while exercising, "I'm burning a lot of calories. While I'm exercising, my body is changing into a better butter-burning machine. The purpose of my exercise is to change my body chemistry. I need a tune-up and that's why I'm exercising. My muscles are getting lean and slinky."
- Combine a steady regimen of aerobic and anaerobic exercise in your program.
- Increase your carbohydrate consumption but eat only the more complex variety. Don't eat fat, because you are what you eat. If you eat a diet high in fat, you can expect to gain fat.

- Switch exercises to avoid overdeveloping some muscles at the expense of others.
- Eat a low-fat diet to reduce the amount of fat that must be burned. To gain muscle mass, train anaerobically through heavy weight training with low repetitions. Then train aerobically to oxygenate the fat and lose the fat, which is the unwanted weight.

Almost all diets prey on the misconception that it is hard to burn fat. Wrong, it is easy! The ultimate cure for obesity is aerobic exercise combined with anaerobic exercise and a low-fat diet. One can never win at the weight-loss game by dieting without exercising.

6

Practice Organization

*"No coach ever won a game by what he knows.
It's what his players have learned."*
—Amos Alonzo Stagg

P aul Richards, former manager of Baltimore Orioles, once said, "Tell a ballplayer something a thousand times, then tell him again, because that might be the time he'll understand something."

The key to success is the way we practice. Because baseball is a game of instinct, we must practice so that we train our bodies to react automatically. Organize in advance with a plan for success, because if you don't, you have a plan for failure. Because the opponent will attack the weakest point of a team, practice eliminating weaknesses. Use the whole-part-whole method of instruction when you develop a yearly practice plan.

When you develop a philosophy for practice, consider these five concepts: find inspirational models you admire, train in a pleasant atmosphere, view practice as fun, set goals for every practice session, and reward a job well done.

When first teaching fundamentals, the most effective instruction is repetitive, offered at a slow, rhythmic pace with every movement done with precision. When teaching players to perform the activity, movements should be executed at full speed.

Safety

Injury prevention results from caring for others. It is always better to prevent an injury than repair the damage. This means you will never have to say, "I'm sorry."

- Batters must wear helmets during all batting drills, in or on deck, and on the base paths.
- Catchers must wear full equipment in the bullpen and during batting practice.
- Use the pitcher's L-shaped screen and the first-base screen. Use an outfield screen as a collection site for batting-practice balls.
- Stop all throws to a base if a runner is there.
- Playing the batted ball to first or second is not permitted.
- Play pepper away from others.
- Players must not play catch near the bench.

Nine Components of a Daily Practice Plan

A solid daily practice includes nine components. Each step is important and should be used. The steps include: warming-up and stretching, on field warm-up, reviewing old skills, learning new skills, practicing game situations, ending practice, conditioning, cool-down and stretching, and evaluating.

Warm-Up and Stretching

Always begin with a cardiovascular activity. We begin with one lap around the field, including javelin arm circles. Next work on calisthenics: 70 push-ups; 25 twisting curl-ups; 10 hyperextensions of the back; 30 butt-ups with palms in, out, and back; 25 twisting curl-ups; 10 squat thrusts; and 50 lunges. Third, perform the seven-minute flexibility program, which embraces the fundamentals of static stretching.

We advocate static stretching, as opposed to ballistic or proprioceptive neuromuscular facilitation (PNF) stretching, because of safety concerns. Ballistic stretching during warm-ups is often associated with muscle strains and related injuries, reduced flexibility, and postactivity pain. PNF stretching demands mature, responsible athletes who communicate carefully. Some say that PNF stretching is the most effective method, but we feel it presents an unnecessary risk for baseball players. Static stretching requires the player to stretch the muscle beyond its normal length. This method involves moving to a position just short of discomfort and holding the stretch for 15 to 25 seconds. As the word *static* implies, no movement should occur during the stretch. Athletes must focus on form and body position to ensure that they are stretching targeted body parts. Attention to balance is another concern, related to both self-control and safety.

STANDING TOE TOUCH

STANDING STRADDLE STRETCH

SEATED STRAIGHT-LEG STRETCH

SEATED TWISTS LEFT

Repeat to the right side.

SEATED SHOULDER STRETCH

SEATED STRADDLE STRETCH TO THE MIDDLE AND LEFT

Repeat to the right side.

LEG TUCKS TO THE CHEST, LEFT, AND RIGHT

Repeat with the right leg.

HIPS-UP STRETCH

LONG AND TALL FULL-BODY STRETCH

PLYOMETRIC DOUBLE-LEG HOPS

On-Field Warm-Up

1. Players run at a slow pace with total concentration on technique.
2. Players throw and catch to warm up their arms. Playing catch is a sport-specific baseball activity that players must be able to perform to play the game. Players should demonstrate proper technique, concentration, dedication, and hustle.

Guidelines for Playing Throw and Catch

1. Players pair up by positions.
   - Pitchers are to alternate various fastball and change-up grips.
   - Infielders are to practice quick-feet and quick-hand development.
   - Outfielders are to practice the high-knee crow hop.
   - Catchers are to warm up on the infield to develop quick hands and quick release.
2. For safety, everyone should throw in the same direction.
3. Players should not talk because we want to create an atmosphere of concentration and intensity.
4. Players should start at about 45 feet apart and finish with a long toss of about 200 feet. The long toss should be a low, hard throw rather than a high, soft throw.
5. Players should always give targets to indicate that they are ready to receive the throw.
6. Balls above the waist are caught with the fingers up.
7. Balls below the waist are caught with the fingers down.

Reviewing Previously Learned Skills

Practicing previously learned skills are an important aspect of practive. It provides a continuity to the "big picture" of player development. It also offers the coach the chance to evaluate his instruction and the players' learning. It automatically puts the all-important component of repetition into the learning process.

Specialty Period for Learning New Skills

The specialty period is the time for teaching and learning new skills by working in small groups. By creating small learning groups you can concentrate on the individual skills of specific positions (e.g, pitchers, catchers, infielders, and outfielders). Or by grouping several different position players together you can work on some team plays. For example, pitchers-catchers first baseman could work on fielding ground balls and covering first base, the middle infielders could practice the double play at second base while the third baseman and outfielders take batting practice in the hitting tunnel. This allows for a very efficient use of practice time by focusing the instruction on only those players who need to learn a specific skill or technique.

Play with a purpose.

Pitchers

Pitchers are the center of the infield, therefore most of the action starts with them. Use these skills to prepare pitchers for the action.

1. Fielding ground balls and throwing to first base
2. Fielding ground balls and throwing to second base while catchers drill on pickoffs
3. Fielding bunts to the first-base line and throwing to second base or first base

4. Fielding bunts to the third-base line and throwing to third base or first base
5. Trapping a popped-up sacrifice bunt, with the intent to confuse the base runner so that he can be forced out
6. Working on wild-pitch and passed-ball defense with the catcher
7. Practicing rundown plays with the infielders
8. Fielding fly balls

Catchers

Catchers are known as the coach on the field, therefore their presence and skills must be sharp and ready at all times.

1. Stances
2. Dry framing
3. Live framing
4. Blocking pitches
5. Shadowing another catcher to develop quickness
6. Throwing to first second and third bases for pick-offs and steals
7. Fielding bunts near home plate and throwing to the bases
8. Catching pop flies
9. Sweeping and punching out the runner on the tag play
10. Wild-pitch and passed-ball defense
11. Tennis-ball catching with the bare hand
12. Force-play double play (1-2-3)

Infielders

Infielders must move quickly and be constantly alert to any situation. The following points are great things for any infielder to practice.

1. Stationary stances—single-handed catching of ground balls, two-handed alligator technique, midline backhand catching of ground balls, forehand (glove-side) ground balls
2. Practicing the funnel technique by incorporating the feet and throwing—funneling the ground ball with two hands to the belly button while moving through the ball to throw
3. Playing the short hop or big hop while fielding ground balls, thereby avoiding the in-between hop that leads to errors
4. Making the play on a slowly hit ground ball
5. Bad-hop drill, seated—dead, rolled, and bounced
6. Diving for ground ball drills—from the prone position glove side, from the prone position with the back hand, from the knees, and from the standing position

7. Catching fly balls
8. Practicing the double play

Outfielders

Outfielders have to be patient in waiting for a play but nevertheless their positions require them to be constantly watchful and prepared as any hit might be hit to them.

1. Stances and drop steps
2. Mass drill—with the following coaching commands, "Ready, go back, move in to catch, two hands, a high-knee crow hop, simulate a throw to home plate, then finish with three hops."
3. Catching fly balls—left and right
4. Wrong-way fly balls—deliberately turn the wrong way and adjust
5. Line drives (hard and soft) off a fungo bat
6. Sliding catch sit-downs
7. Fence packages (fly balls, CNN Catch of the Day, ground balls off the fence, three-ball drills, two-man drills)
8. Fielding ground balls—the infield technique for safety when runners are not advancing, the all-or-none technique when the runner must be thrown out, the down-the-line technique when throwing the runner out at second base
9. Cutoff throws to infielders
10. Relay throws to either the shortstop or the second baseman

Hitters

Batters initiate the offensive play once the pitch has been thrown. Try these exercises for making every at bat the best shot for scoring as possible.

1. Bunting
2. Hitting in batting cages for batting practice

Team Defense

Practice running defensive plays in small groups.

1. One-throw rundown play
2. Bunt defenses
3. Pickoff plays
4. First-and-third defensive plays
5. Forced balk defense
6. Wild-pitch and passed-ball defense
7. Fly-ball protocol

8. Pitchout with the slide step
9. Cutoff plays
10. Relay plays

Multiple Drills

1. Multiple pickoff drills with rundown. Use three pitchers, two short-stops, two second basemen, one first baseman, and one catcher. See chapter 11 for examples.
2. Multiple relay drill. Use a full team, with three outfielders, a short-stop, a second baseman, and a pitcher ready to rotate into the drill on the next fungoed ball. Hit the fungo ball down the lines and then in the power alleys for a sure double and possible triple.

Practicing Game Situations in a Large Group

1. Start with the pregame outfield and infield drill. Remember these points as you start:

- Catchers should wear their full equipment and throw from behind home plate.
- Infielders and catchers should target the chest of the receiver.
- On cutoff throws outfielders should target the infielders' knees.
- Pitchers should work from the mound with first-baseman plays.

Tables 6.1 and 6.2 shows the various phases of this drill for infielders and outfielders.

2. Next go to batting practice and baserunning. During batting practice, fungo ground balls are hit to the infielders during the time between pitches thrown to the batter. Normally we have two fungo hitters, one on each side of home plate. The fungo hitter on the first-base side hits to either the third baseman or the second baseman. The fungo hitter on the third-base side hits to either the shortstop or the first baseman. These fungo ground balls are played to either first or second base. The catching and throwing therefore stimulate the entire defensive play.

Occasionally, hit fungo fly balls to the outfielders. By placing the outfielders in left and right fields and a simple relay team in foul territory, we can hit, catch, and throw the ball in a figure-8 pattern.

3. Ask pitchers to do their normal workout from the mound with gamelike performance. To facilitate practice, an extra pitcher backs up the mound to feed baseballs to the pitcher. We ask the pitcher to throw hard, throw strikes, and tell the hitter what type of pitch is coming.

- Round 1. The batter executes a sacrifice bunt with a runner on first base. With the runner still at second base the batter uses one pitch to attempt to bunt for a hit. Meanwhile the runner is checking the outfielder's position. With the runner on third base the

Table 6.1 Outfielders' Phase

Round	Reps	Position	Speed of ball	Type	Ball direction	Play procedure
1	1	LF	Hard hit	Line drive	LF corner	Relay to SS
	1	LF-CF	Hard hit	Line drive	LCF	Relay to SS
	1	CF-RF	Hard hit	Line drive	RCF	Relay to 2b
	1	RF	Hard hit	Line drive	RF corner	Relay to 2b
2	3	LF	Hard hit	G.B.*	Down the line	Throw to 2nd
	3	CF	Hard hit	G.B.	Directly**	Throw to 3rd
	3	RF	Hard hit	Short fly ball	Directly	Throw to 3rd
3	2	LF	Hard hit	G.B.	Directly	Throw to home
	1	LF	Soft hit	Short fly ball	Directly	Throw to home
	2	CF	Hard hit	G.B.	Directly	Throw to home
	1	CF	Soft hit	Short fly ball	Directly	Throw to home
	2	RF	Hard hit	G.B.	Directly	Throw to home
	1	RF	Soft hit	Short fly ball	Directly	Throw to home

*G.B. = ground ball
**Directly = hit ball directly to the player

Table 6.2 Infielders' Phase

Round	Depth	Position	Speed of ball	Type	Ball direction	Play procedure	Throw around procedure
1	Up	3B	Normal	G.B.	Directly	5-2 tag	none
	Up	SS	Normal	G.B.	Directly	6-2 tag	none
	Up	2B	Normal	G.B.	Directly	4-2 tag	none
	Up	1B	Normal	G.B.	Directly	3-2 tag	none
2	Normal	3B	Normal	G.B.	Directly	5-3	2-5-4-3-2
		SS	Normal	G.B.	Directly	6-3	2-6-5-2
		2B	Normal	G.B.	Directly	4-3	2-4-5-2
		1B	Normal	G.B.	Directly	3-1	none

Round	Depth	Position	Speed of ball	Type	Ball direction	Play procedure	Throw around procedure
	Inbox	C	Slow	Bunt	First baseline	2-3	2-6-5-2
3		3B	Normal	G.B.	To infielder's left	5-3	2-5-4-3-2
		SS	Normal	G.B.	To infielder's left	6-3	2-6-5-2
		2B	Normal	G.B.	To infielder's left	4-3	2-4-5-2
		1B	Normal	G.B.	To infielder's left	3-1	none
	In box	C	Slow	Bunt	Third baseline	2-3	6-5-2
4		3B	Normal	G.B.	To infielder's right	5-3	2-5-4-3-2
		SS	Normal	G.B.	To infielder's right	6-3	2-6-5-2
		2B	Normal	G.B.	To infielder's right	4-3	2-4-5-2
		1B	Normal	G.B.	To infielders right	3-1	none
	In box	C	Slow	Bunt	Third baseline	2-3	6-5-2
		3B	Normal	G.B.	To infielder's right	5-3	2-5-4-3-2
		SS	Normal	G.B.	To infielder's right	6-3	2-6-5-2
		2B	Normal	G.B.	To infielder's right	4-3	2-4-5-2
		1B	Normal	G.B.	To infielder's right	3-1	none
	In box	C	Slow	Strike out	Foul territory	2-3	6-5-2
5	DP	3B	Normal	G.B.	To 3B right	5-4-3	2-5-2
	DP	SS	Normal	G.B.	To SS right	6-4-3	2-6-2

(continued)

Table 6.2 (continued)

Round	Depth	Position	Speed of ball	Type	Ball direction	Play procedure	Throw around procedure
	DP	32B	Normal	G.B.	To 2B right	4-6-3	2-4-2
	DP	1B	Normal	G.B.	To 1B right	3-6-1	none
	In box	C	Slow	Bunt	In front of	3-6-3	none
6	DP	3B	Normal	G.B.	To 3B	5-4-3	2-5-2
	DP	SS	Normal	G.B.	To SS	6-4-3	2-6-2
	DP	2B	Normal	G.B.	To 2B	4-6-3	2-4-2
	DP	1B	Normal	G.B.	To 1B	3-6-1	none
	In box	C	Slow	Bunt	Front of mate	2-6-3	none
7	DP	3B	Hard	G.B.	Down the line	5-3	none
	Normal	3B	Slow	G.B.	Directly	5-3	none
	Up	3B	Normal	G.B.	Directly	5-2-3	none
	DP	SS	Hard	G.B.	In the hole	6-3	none
	Normal	SS	Slow	G.B.	Over the mound	6-3	none
	Up	SS	Normal	G.B.	Directly	6-2-3	none
	DP	2B	Hard	G.B.	Up the middle	4-3	none
	Normal	2B	Slow	G.B.	Directly	4-3	none
	Up	2B	Normal	G.B.	Directly	4-2-3	none
	DP	1B	Normal	G.B.	Directly	3-5	none
	Up	1B	Slow	Bunt	Directly	3-5	none
	Up	1B	Slow	G.B.	Directly	3-2	none
	In box	C	Hard	Pop-up	Foul territory	2	NA

batter tries to hit a ground ball for a hit. The batter then takes five swings or any reasonable combination of swings. When the coach determines the end of the batter's practice, the batter-runner runs to first base. As he touches first base he turns his head to the right to develop the habit of looking for the overthrow at first base. The runner at first should learn to advance properly on a sacrifice bunt. The runner takes a normal primary lead at first base and on the pitch extends it to a secondary lead. He advances only when the batter bunts the ball on the ground.

When he reaches second base the runner immediately checks the positioning and depth of the outfielders. The objective is to learn to score from second base on a line drive without turning to look to the outfield. This occurs at the same time the batter is attempting to bunt for a hit.

At second base the runner takes a normal 17-foot lead and extends it on the pitch to a secondary lead. Here he must learn to advance instinctively on base hits, wild pitches, and passed balls. He advances on ground balls by using the rule of thumb. On fly balls he should go halfway. We do not want him to tag up on fly balls. At third base he takes the lead in foul territory so that he is not out if a batted ball hits him. The primary lead should be as long as the pitcher and third baseman permit. On the windup the runner should use the three-step walking lead to build momentum. Here he must learn to react quickly. If the ball is hit in the air the rule is to tag up on all line drives and fly balls. If the ball is hit on the ground he should break for home. If, however, he will be a sure out at the plate, he should change up and get into a rundown play, staying in the rundown long enough to allow the batter to advance to second base.

- Round 2. This time try executing the New York Yankees' routine. On the first pitch the batter and runner practice the hit-and-run play. The batter should look for a bad pitch because he must protect the runner.

  On the second pitch they execute a suicide-squeeze play. The key to this play is for the runner to start and the batter to show a bunt as the pitcher's front foot hits the ground.

  Then the batter takes five swings or any reasonable combination of swings. The coach ends the batter's turn by saying, "Next hitter."

4. Make sure the defense catches all fly balls during batting practice.

5. Practice additional base-running drills during "pro BP" to work on breaks and leads from each base.

   - At first base—one-way lead, indirect steal, delayed steal, double steal, two-out play, delayed double steal, force balk, and the hit-and-run

- At third base—suicide squeeze, safety squeeze, delayed squeeze, straight steal of home, double steal, fake suicide squeeze and steal of second

Ending Practice

End practice by playing modified games or performing play-specific drills. Intrasquad games, coach-directed fungo games, and players hitting with modified pitching are examples of this component. Sometimes we readjust the ball-and-strike count by dropping the ball count and keeping the strikes when a batter gets four balls. Or players may pitch to their own team to increase the chance of hitting the baseball.

Drills to end practice are designed to allow players to practice under pressure. The idea is to do it once and do it right. For each drill establish an achievable numeric goal. On every failure we restart the count.

Stealing Second Base Vs. Live Pitching and Catchers' Throwing

Purpose: To create a competitive, gamelike situation for the pitcher and catcher versus the runner at first base (see diagram page 95)

Implementation:
1. Place three loose bases on the first-base line, spaced evenly about 3 feet apart. Place three loose bases 90 feet away, spaced evenly about 3 feet apart even with second base.
2. Put a pitcher on the mound in a set position, a catcher behind the plate, and an infielder to cover second base. Their goal is to prevent the steal of second base. They may do anything to hold the runner at first base. The catcher may throw out the runner at second base.
3. Using first base and the three loose bases, put four base runners on the field. Their goal is to avoid being picked off yet get a good lead and break to steal second base successfully.
4. The defense reacts to the front runner, while all four runners react to the pitcher. This drill should be highly competitive. After each "play," a new pitcher and catcher rotate to the position, and four new runners move in at first base.
5. If a runner can steal three consecutive bases, he is finished. If he gets picked off or thrown out, he starts over again with zero.
6. If a catcher throws out three runners, he is finished with practice.
7. For further evaluation, the coach can time the pitcher's delivery, the catcher's throwing time to second base, and the runner's time to second base.

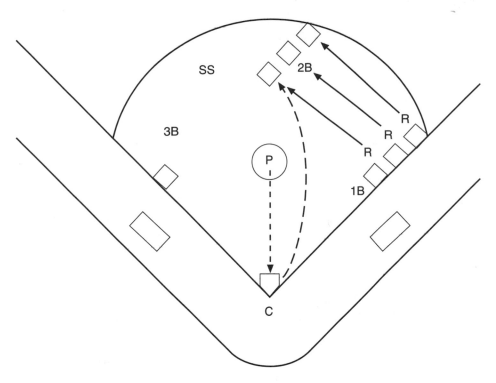

Stealing second base vs. live pitching and catcher's throwing.

21 Fly Balls

Purpose: To teach fly-ball protocol and develop the skill of catching fly balls

Implementation:
1. Divide the ballclub into two equal squads of nine players by position.
2. Put nine players (one team) on the field at their positions.
3. The coach hits either high balls or pop flies. It best to attempt to hit them in the areas between three players. Players must use the proper protocol and then catch the ball for an out. After three outs change teams just as in a game.
4. The first team to catch 21 fly balls in a row (seven innings) is done with practice. If a team misses a fly ball they go back to zero and start all over.
5. To make this drill more challenging, do it on a windy day.

Seven Scoreless Innings

Purpose: To teach baseball strategies of how to get out of an inning without allowing a run

Implementation:
1. Divide the ballclub into two equal squads of nine players by position.
2. Put nine players (one team) on the field at their positions, while the other team is at bat and running the bases for the coach.
3. The coach hits fungoes to create any game situation he wants. He should attempt to put the team in pressure situations. Try this sequence: a base hit, a sacrifice bunt to move the runner to second base, a ground-ball single between shortstop and third base to create a first-and-third situation, then a ground ball back to the pitcher to create a 1-6-3 double play to end the inning.
4. As in a game, the teams change from offense to defense and vice versa after three outs.
5. The first team to complete seven innings is finished with practice. If a defensive team allows a run they return to the first inning and begin again.

Nine Consecutive Base Hits

Purpose: To develop an attitude that hits come in bunches

Implementation:
1. Put eight players in the field by position and have a starting lineup ready to bat in order. Allow anyone to pitch, throwing only fastballs.
2. The batters hit in the predetermined order with the goal of getting nine consecutive base hits. If anyone makes an out, the group goes back to zero to begin again. As the base hits occur, the pressure mounts on the next hitter to keep the rally going.
3. When they get nine consecutive base hits, the practice ends.

Conditioning

Always do your conditioning last (see table 6.3).

Table 6.3	**Conditioning Chart**			
Monday	**Tuesday**	**Wednesday**	**Thursday**	**Friday**
6×100yd, $^1/_2$ speed	10×10 DB knee hops	1 mile run	10×10 DB knee hops	$^1/_2$ mile runs
	6×6 bases	walk lap	3×90	3×360, $^1/_2$ speed
		1 mile run	3×180	10 starts
			3×270	
			3×360	
Monday	**Tuesday**	**Wednesday**	**Thursday**	**Friday**
1 mile jog	1 mile jog	$^1/_2$ mile run	1 mile jog	$^1/_2$ mile run
3×10 bases	5×100 form	4 starts	5×90	3 HR trots
	$^1/_2$ mile jog	4 steals	5×180	10 starts
			5×270	
			5×360	

Cool-Down and Stretching

Coaches often neglect the stretching and cool-down component of practice. Sports-medicine experts believe that this activity is important in preventing injury and promoting recovery. I recommend combining cool-down and stretching with an evaluation period at the end of practice.

Evaluation of Practice by Players and Coach

Always evaluate performance with the tool of quality control. Practice itself is not enough; it must be intelligent practice that has self-improvement as its goal.

Indoor Practice

Baseball is designed to be play outdoors. Make every effort to practice outside. Sometimes, when the weather is bad, however, practice must be moved indoors. When this happens practice is limited by facility size, scheduling conflicts, availability of equipment, and so on. Practicing indoors, however, lends itself to better individual skill instruction.

When practicing indoors you should still use the nine components of a daily practice plan that we cited earlier in this chapter. Devote most of the practice time to the three components involving teaching and learning—previously learned skills, a specialty period for learning new skills, and practicing modified game situations. Warm-up and stretching, on-field warm-up, conditioning, cool-down and stretching, and the practice-ending evaluation remain much the same.

For defensive skill instruction, form four groups of players by position—pitchers, infielders, outfielders, and catchers. These groups sometimes combine to work on particular plays. For example, pitchers and infielders may work on pickoff plays.

Batting practice indoors without netting is a problem that we have solved by hitting tennis balls, Wiffle balls, or socks. Safety is an issue that must be addressed because of the close quarters of most facilities. L-shaped screens are necessary safety equipment.

If space is limited try to acquire a classroom with a VCR. By rotating various groups between the gym and the classroom, you can maximize instruction. I've often shown instructional videos and rules videos to a group of players while other groups are in the gym working out.

Finally, note the windchill-factor chart, which provides both players and coaches with an objective measure of the danger of outdoor practice in cold weather.

Speed in MPH	Equivalent temperature in Farenheit											
Calm	50	40	30	20	10	0	-10	-20	-30	-40	-50	-60
5	46	37	27	16	6	-5	-15	-26	-36	-47	-57	-66
10	40	28	16	4	-9	-24	-33	-46	-58	-70	-83	-98
15	36	22	9	-5	-18	-32	-45	-58	-72	-85	-99	-119
20	32	18	4	-10	-25	-39	-53	-67	-82	-96	-110	-125
25	30	16	0	-15	-29	-44	-59	-74	-88	-104	-118	-154
30	28	13	-2	-18	-33	-48	-63	-79	-94	-109	-125	-140
35	27	11	-4	-20	-35	-51	-67	-82	-98	-113	-129	-144
40	26	10	-6	-21	-37	-53	-69	-85	-100	-116	-132	-149
	Green				Yellow			Red				

Wind speeds greater than 40 MPH have little additional effect.

Green: Little danger for properly clothed personnel, maximum danger of a false sense of security
Yellow: Increasing danger from freezing of exposed flesh.
Red: Great danger.

Windchill-factor chart.

Amos Alonzo Stagg said, "No coach has ever won a game by what he knows. Rather games are won by what and how much his players have learned." Sometimes after a poor performance coaches say, "I told them how to do that!" However, it isn't what they were told, but what they learned to do in practice! Ball players will demonstrate their grasp of the coach's instructions by their performance.

7

Pitching

"Work fast, change speeds, and throw strikes."
—*Ray Miller*

T he great Connie Mack once stated that pitching is 75 percent of the game. Others concede it to be 65 percent to 85 percent of winning baseball. No matter the percentage, pitching is the most important factor in producing a winning team.

To pitch effectively, the pitcher must have command—of both himself and his pitches. This asset is crucial because the pitcher starts every play. Another way to express the idea is that the pitcher must be in control—of his emotions, of all his pitches, and of his body so that he has good balance.

Anger is the pitcher's main enemy. It can even affect the delicate workings of a great pitcher in a close ballgame. No constructive thought can come out of anger. It is an inexcusable affliction. As soon as he loses control of himself, the pitcher will lose control of the ball.

To be a consistent winner, a pitcher must start with the following ideas:

1. "Work fast, change speeds, and throw strikes," says former major-league pitching coach Ray Miller. Studies show that images and thoughts remain in muscle memory for 10 to 11 seconds. Thus, the idea is to work fast enough that the batter cannot mentally replay a failed attempt at a pitch. The pitcher should not give the batter a chance to prepare to hit.

2. Pitchers must learn to throw first-pitch strikes. More advanced pitchers learn to pitch to spots.

3. Pitchers should analyze the hitter's strengths and weaknesses. They must be willing to chart pitches, watch the opponent's batting practice, and scout games. Before pitching to an unknown hitter, the pitcher should watch the hitter's practice swings.

4. By knowing how to field his position, the pitcher becomes a useful fifth infielder. Because the pitcher is so close to the batter, he must know how to protect himself as a fielder.

5. The pitcher should have confidence in himself and his team, and be willing to show it, especially by challenging hitters. He should feel that if he doesn't get them, someone else will.

6. Keeping the body in great physical condition, especially the legs, is essential. Many experts believe that the pitcher is only as good as his legs. The pitcher must do both strength training and aerobic training if he expects to excel.

Pitching Mechanics

Proper technique and conditioning are the keys to protecting the throwing arm. Proper mechanics and control are, in effect, one and the same.

The problem of throwing a baseball is one of building power and imparting it to the baseball. Accuracy, however, is also crucial. Maximum speed is not always essential; a change of pace or direction is often better.

Remember that proper rhythm and timing are the basics of successful pitching. All smooth pitchers start with a slow windup. The tempo is slow, slow, slow, and then fast. The pitcher should place the ball deep in the glove so that the entire pitching hand and wrist are in the glove. Wrists should face each other with each pitch to prevent tipping off the pitch to the hitter.

Concentration is necessary. Lack of concentration will cause the pitcher to be wild inside versus a right-handed hitter. To produce good control, all pitches must break in a downward plane. Therefore, two deliveries are correct, overhead and three quarter; both require the elbows to be kept up. In addition, the closer the hand comes to the head at the point of release, the greater the mechanical advantage.

The longer the arm, the greater the hand speed and the greater the velocity and movement. Short arming is a common fault. To increase arm length, the palm must be down as the arm is extended. Another common fault is incomplete extension of the arm in windup. This results in less force imparted to the baseball because of the smaller arc and the shorter distance through which the arm moves. The elbows must be up at shoulder level or above. The pitcher should lead with his nose, front elbow, and front knee. He should shift his eyes and fine-focus on the target, which should be the catcher's glove. Fine focusing means having a clear, sharp concentration on the target. Then the pitcher must think low and pitch down.

Seven Pitching Checkpoints

There are seven steps to focus on while pitching. Follow the guidelines listed here.

Point One

• *From the Windup.* The posture should be such that the head is in front of the belly button directly over the pivot foot with the body weight on the nonpivot foot. While slowly shifting the weight to pivot the foot front of the body, whether he lifts over the head or under the chin, the pitcher takes a short step

Wind-up position.

Set position.

directly back and away from home plate, then steps to place the pivot foot against the front side of the rubber. All the while he maintains a posture with the head directly over the pivot foot. The hands stay close to the body.

• *From the Set Position.*The feet are spread about shoulder-width apart with a staggered foot position so that the front heel is aligned with the pivot-foot toe. The hands are together and slightly above the belly button with the elbows flexed and relaxed at 90 degrees. Again, the head is in front of the belly button.

Point Two: Primary Balance Position

The pitcher slowly lifts the knee to a position parallel to the ground with the toe pointing down. He should be especially careful not to swing the leg. The hands are in a praying position. The eyes should be level, looking directly at the target. The hips and shoulders are turned together, slightly showing the hip pocket to the catcher. At this point a slight pause occurs. When the knee reaches its highest point, the pitcher pulls the ball from the glove with the thumbs going down toward the ground.

Point Three: Secondary Balance Position

The hands break with the thumbs pointing downward and the elbows moving into a flexed-T position so that both elbows are at shoulder height. The ball comes out of the glove downward, backward, and up to a flexed-elbow position facing second base. For directional purposes, the elbow, nose, and front knee point directly toward

Primary balance position.

Secondary balance position.

the target as the pitcher strides toward home plate. The head holds still and leads to the target with the hip. The pitcher does not flex the back leg until the leg lift starts down from the primary balance point. The stride foot lands on the ball of the foot. While sitting slightly on the back leg, the pitcher shows the ball extended toward second base simultaneously with front-foot landing. The front foot stays closed while stepping about two inches across the line between the back point of home plate and the instep of the back foot.

Point Four: Weight Transfer and Late Rotation

The fourth checkpoint is the only one that occurs in motion. The pitcher transfers the weight from the ball of the pivot foot to the ball of the stride foot, then rotates late. The object is to keep the shoulder closed as long as possible before rotating late. The hip and shoulders rotate and simultaneously square up with the plate. A powerful abdominal flexion occurs. The elbow leads the throwing arm with the hand flexed at 130 to 160 degrees. The shoulders are off level at about 20 to 30 degrees, with the throwing side higher. The lead elbow pulls down toward the hip but is never allowed to pass behind the body. At this point, the baseball is in the tennis-serve

Transferring the weight and rotating around.

Third balance position.

position with the ball at the highest point.

At the release point the pivot foot rolls over onto the laces, forcing the hip to snap at the same time the body follows through with the arm. The body slightly hyperextends at the waist. To develop extra power, the pitchers pulls the back knee forward and slightly inward to get the back hip forward. This is the back-knee drive.

Point Five: Third Balance Position

At this point the belly button should be over the knee with the pitching hand reaching for the catcher's glove. The goal is to be long in the front. The head must be in line with eyes level. The pivot foot is now off the ground. It is especially important not to overrotate.

Point Six: Over the Barrel

While the back foot kicks over the barrel, the back foot should be visible over the top of the head when viewed from home plate. The pitching arm should dangle in front of the front leg. It is important that both elbows remain in front of the body. Now the pivot foot lands.

Point Seven: Fielding Position

The stride foot steps up to square the body to the plate. The hands come up in the defensive position. The pitcher is now an infielder. Remember, every pitcher (even in the major leagues) will eventually de-

Over the barrel.

Fielding position.

velop mechanical faults. The responsibility of pitching coaches is to help pitchers maintain solid mechanics. Working on mechanics is an endless challenge.

Location and Rotation

Two of the keys to making a quality pitch are location and rotation movement. The pitcher doesn't want a straight pitch. In general, location means throwing the ball in the direction of the target. Location is required to make a quality pitch. For example, if a running inside movement is desired, the pitcher should throw to the inside half of the plate, and the winning fastball must be thrown down.

Another key to pitching success lies in the pitcher's ability to throw the ball in a downward plane. This means that the ball follows a downward trajectory from the point of release to home plate. Pitching on a downward plane means that the ball is moving in two planes, forward and downward.

The batter swings the bat in a single plane parallel to the ground. If the pitcher throws sidearm, the fastball will travel in the same plane as the bat. Likewise, the sidearm curveball will break flat and remain in the same plane. The ball that travels in two planes will be more difficult to hit.

The baseball rotates 14 to 16 times between the pitcher's mound and home plate, no matter how fast it is propelled. Obviously, 16 rotations are preferred. Getting better spin on the ball is one of the surest ways to improve pitching. If the ball is thrown in the direction of the desired break and spin (rotation) is maximized, excellent movement can be obtained.

In throwing the various pitches, the pitcher should pay close attention to velocity. Changing speeds is a major factor in successful pitching. By varying each pitch significantly, the pitcher can confuse the hitter's timing.

Fastball

The average major-league speed is 85 to 87 miles per hour. Our recommended age for learning to throw a fastball is between 6 and 10 years old.

Fastball grip.

Atlanta Braves pitching coach Leo Mazzone stressed the importance of establishing the fastball on the outside corner early in the game. When the pitcher does this, hitters must respect the fastball and cannot sit back for the breaking ball.

Pitchers should learn both the two-seam fastball and the four-seam fastball. The four-seam fastball travels three to four miles per hour faster than the two-seamer. The slower two-seam fastball sinks three inches more than the four-seamer before it reaches the plate. If the pitcher can develop two fastballs with different velocity and movement, he obviously has two different pitches.

The pitcher grips the ball with last joint of the forefinger, middle finger, and thumb so that a space is created. He attempts to get the ball out in the fingers and away from the palm. Generally, the farther out into the fingers he grips the baseball, the greater the speed. Conversely, the farther back toward the palm of the hand he grips the baseball, the slower the speed. Therefore, the pitcher should not choke the ball when throwing the fastball.

For better movement and life on the ball, the pitcher can experiment with grip and delivery. He can drop down to the three-quarter delivery or try using index-finger pressure. He should use a grip with the two seams of the ball (known as the point of the ball) when throwing away from the arm and a grip across the four seams when throwing over the top or sidearm.

The pitcher should relax his wrist as he comes back to get a wrist snap. The snap of the wrist and the natural pronation of the wrist cause the ball to spin, which promotes movement. Getting better spin on the ball is one of the surest ways to pitch-

Fastball grip with the choke.

ing improvement. To get the most effective spin, the release must be directly behind the baseball. The pitcher should try not to "cut" the ball. By cutting the ball, he may create some movement but speed will decrease. The 216 raised red cotton stitches that hold together the baseball's leather cover create uneven airflow over the surface of the ball. As a result, the ball is pulled in the direction of the seam.

Over the long haul, throwing is the best way to develop arm strength. Pitchers should play long toss during the off-season two or three times a week. Throwing a weighted baseball to develop arm strength is a proven training method. Some successful pitchers squeeze a rubber ball to strengthen their fingers.

Slider

The average major-league speed is 81 to 82 miles per hour. Our recommended age for learning to throw a slider is between 14 and 18 years old.

The slider is a hard breaking ball that appears to the hitter to be a fastball but at the last split second breaks sharply four to six inches in a direction opposite the fastball movement. The spin should be a tight, football-like spiral, creating a small red dot visible to both the catcher and the pitcher.

The pitchers should not choke the ball because doing so will decrease velocity. The ball should be held slightly off center to enhance spin. With a loose wrist the pitcher should throw the ball hard so that it looks like a fastball. The slider should be thrown off the fastball rather than off the curveball. The pitchers should think "fastball, fastball, slider" as he throws, keeping the ball down by throwing in a downward plane. At the last instant he quickly supinates the loose wrist and releases the ball off the tip of the middle finger. It is helpful to point the index finger at home plate.

The right-handed pitcher can effectively throw the backup slider to left-handed hitters on the outside corner. The left-handed pitcher can throw the backup or backdoor slider to right-handed hitters.

Slider grip.

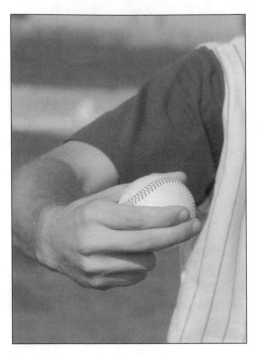

Standard curveball grip.

Curveball

The average major-league speed is 68 to 72 miles per hour. Our recommended age to learn to throw a curveball is between 12 and 16 years old.

The more spin the pitcher puts on a ball, the more it will curve. Also, the slower the speed, the more it tends to curve. The pitcher should not try to make the ball curve; he should make it spin. He must never overthrow the curveball.

Again, the pitcher should not choke the ball when he grips it. He should put pressure on the middle finger and thumb; however, if he gets a slider rotation, he should choke the ball a little to achieve better downward rotation.

The pitcher should preset the wrist when he extends the arm after the hand break. He doesn't extend the wrist or wrap the wrist. He must be sure to keep the elbows up and parallel to the shoulder in the flexed-T position.

Curveball grip with the turn.

Curveball at the release.

A common mistake is rushing the primary balance position. This premature weight shift will cause a hanging curveball, a curve that is neither spun sharply enough to make it drop nor thrown correctly in a downward plane. The pitcher should keep the weight back over the rear foot so that he can get on top of the ball. The idea is to throw the thumb at the catcher. To get on top, the pitcher may want to shorten his stride.

The key to the curve is having the proper axis of rotation, that is, being as horizontal as possible. The side of the pitching hand must come through first, then pulled hard, like a shade, without a wrist snap. The curve must be thrown downward in the direction the pitch should break. The pitcher should not be afraid to throw it for a ball.

As the pitcher turns his hips and shoulders, his hand should already be in the proper position, with the back of his fingers toward the catcher. The arm should not be extended but kept bent as long as possible. The follow-through takes the hand and arm to the opposite knee.

Strategically, a left-hander should throw an overhand curve to a right-handed hitter, and a right-handed pitcher can throw an overhand curve to a left-handed hitter. A three-quarter curve is effective right on right and left on left.

Change-Up

The recommended age to learn to throw a change-up is between 12 and 16 years old. The purpose of the change-up is to upset the hitter's timing.
Change-ups are not calculated to strike out hitters. They are designed to reduce the power of the hitter by upsetting the rhythm of his swing.

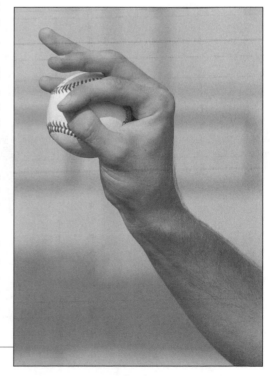

The key to the change-up is maintaining a good motion. Good motion with a bad change is better than a good change. The change-up looks like a fastball but isn't. The pitcher should learn to throw one good change-up. He can experiment with various grips, such as the three-finger fastball, a "choked" fastball, an OK change, a slip pitch, a pitchfork grip, and a split-finger fastball.

The pitcher should throw the ball hard and downward while maintaining arm speed and allowing the grip to reduce ball speed. On the OK change, he keeps his wrist between the face and the ball. This

OK change.

Slip pitch.

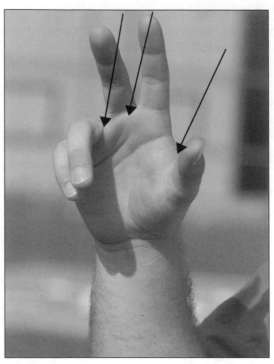

Pressure points for gripping the slip pitch.

Pitchfork grip.

Split-finger fastball.

pitch is effective against good hitters when the logical pitch is the fastball. The OK change isn't useful against poor hitters because it becomes merely a slow ball within the range of their bat speed.

To throw a slower change-up, the pitcher can use any change-up grip and combine that with the pitching mechanics of dragging the pivot foot to lose additional velocity. This combined technique creates a much slower change-up.

Control

Outstanding control is the key to being a winning pitcher. A player must have control of his pitches.

> **Question:** *When is a pitch really a pitch?*
>
> **Answer:** *It is a pitch if the pitcher can throw it for a strike 70 percent of the time and use it at least 20 percent of the time.*
>
> **Question:** *How many corners does a pitcher see?*
>
> **Answer:** *The four corners are up and in, up and away, down and in, and down and away.*

Without control, a pitcher is useless. Successful pitching depends on ball movement and control. But without control, it is impossible to be a pitcher.

To be a winning pitcher, a player must have control of all his pitches. Control is a composite of four factors—concentration, balance, proper ball release, and constant practice. Simply put, all pitching is target practice.

A great start is to visualize the anticipated path or groove of the ball before pitching and to visualize the release point. The player

Focus, concentrate, and aim the ball for the strike.

Cybernetics:
Mental Practice Makes Perfect for Better Control

I believe that each player has an inborn instinct to succeed. It seems logical that everyone should use this positive aspect of players' minds to improve performance. The concept is that the nervous system cannot distinguish what is real from what is imagined.

The basic principles of this approach to cybernetics are simple. A positive self-image is the key to ability and performance. It sets boundaries for what a player can and cannot do; positive thinking, however, may clash with a self-image. The player must see himself as successful. If he doesn't see himself as succeeding, chances are that nobody else will.

Improve the player's self-image and you will improve his performances, both successes and failures. Success will come more frequently, while the frequency of failure will decline.

The mind does not always know the difference between what is real and what is imagined. A creative imagination can overcome the reality of physical performance, because a mind once touched by a new idea never regains its original dimensions. Programming a player for success is simple. Instruct your players in the following two-step process.

1. **Establish clear goals.** Know where you want to go, how you are going to get there, and when you expect to get there. Once you get started in the direction of your goals, nothing can stop you.

2. **Develop a creative imagination.** Allow your mind to show mental pictures to improve performance. Just close your eyes and let it happen. Envision yourself doing it right, doing it well, and winning.

---

can talk to himself on the mound before he pitches. For example, he can say "low and outside" repeatedly.

The pitcher should have no fear about hitting the batter because if the batter is hit he will laugh all the way to first base. The pitcher should be assertive, that is, he should get what he wants without hurting the opponent.

The most important pitch is a strike. The first pitch should be a strike that the player can pitch, rather than just throw. Being ahead in the count gives the pitcher the clear advantage in the pitcher–batter confrontation. A .220 hitter ahead in the count will hit .290. The same hitter behind in the count will hit .180.

Pitchers who have a habit of wearing their caps low on their heads may be able to block out distraction by narrowing their area of concentration.

Proper use of the eyes is important in developing control. The pitcher must not watch the ball. Instead, he should look at the target. Rather than using the catcher's glove, he should use the catcher's cup as a target. He should not look at the target too soon and too long but should instead use a fine focus. A common mistake is to look at the batter before releasing the ball. Anger causes the eyes to dance and dart like those of a wild animal; therefore, pitchers must not become angry.

The pitcher should direct his nose, an elbow, and the front knee toward the target. The action is similar to sighting a target down the barrel of a rifle. After the release, the pitcher should attempt to be long armed as he reaches for the catcher's glove. He follows through with the body and follows the ball to the target. Common problems and the simplest correction follow.

Problem	Correction
Too high	Shorten the stride.
Too low	Cut the arm action short. Therefore, the pitcher should adjust arm action by reaching for the catcher's glove.
High and inside	Opened up too soon. Therefore, the pitcher should stay compact and drive the front elbow toward the target.

Strategy

The key philosophical concept is to work fast, throw strikes, and change speeds. Pitchers should learn the inside-outside style of pitching, particularly against hitters who crowd the plate. But they must not be too cute. The inside half of the home plate must belong to the pitcher, when he wants it. To do this, he must develop the skills necessary to tilt the hitter, that is, make him lean away from the plate. The pitcher must make an effort to jam the hitter. Pitching inside means hard stuff on the plate and 4 inches to 12 inches off the plate. Pitches should be tight around the neck and head inside, not with the intent to hit the batter but to make the outside pitches effective. To communicate the location of pitches, we use the zones A through E (see diagram on page 116).

The pitcher should understand that by pitching ahead in the count he has a better percentage against every hitter. With an 0-2 or 1-2 count, he should set up the hitter with a purpose, that is, waste the next pitch. He might throw six inches outside because the umpires set up inside and cannot see it. The next pitch might be up and in at the knob to create the tilt. With the 2-2 count, the pitcher should throw his best pitch, the pitch he sees himself throwing for strikes. This is the time to challenge the hitter with his best stuff, the time to go one on one.

Every pitcher must develop a straight change-up because it is the easiest way to change speeds. But the pitcher should not throw a change-up to a weak hitter. Instead, the pitcher should challenge him.

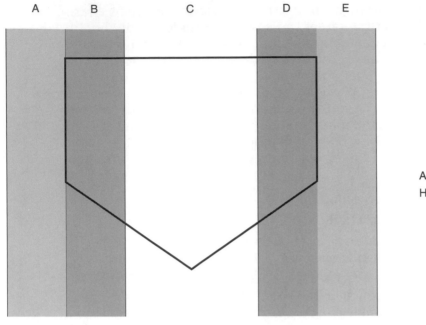

A = 4 inches
B = 4 inches
C = 9 inches
D = 4 inches
E = 4 inches

A baseball is 2 3/4 inches wide.
Home plate is 17 inches wide.

A-E pitching zones.

When behind in the count, the pitcher should not give in to the hitter. He should throw curves and other breaking stuff when behind, provided he has the ability to get the breaking stuff over the plate.

Knowing the Hitter

To be a consistent winner, a pitcher must analyze the hitter's strengths and weaknesses and use that to his advantage. He should use intelligence to pitch to the batter's weakness, especially when ahead in the count. The idea is to make the batter hit a tough pitch. If the hitter is making a mistake, the pitcher should make him pay the price.

Every pitch thrown should be designed to get the batter out. The pitcher should remember that he can't strike anyone out on the first pitch, but he can get an out on the first pitch. Pitchers can use the following ideas about pitching to different kinds of hitters.

1. A right-handed pitcher versus a right-handed batter should use fastballs high and inside, fastballs low and away, or curves low and away.
2. A right-handed pitcher versus a left-handed batter should use fastballs low and outside, curves low and inside, or fastballs high and outside.

3. A left-handed pitcher versus a right-handed batter should use fastballs low and inside, curves low and inside, or fastballs high and outside.
4. A left-handed pitcher versus a left-handed batter should use curves low and away, fastballs up and in, or fastballs low and away.
5. Pitch a pull hitter low and outside with fastballs or curves.
6. Jam the opposite-field hitter with fastballs high and inside.
7. Change speeds and pitch away against the straightaway hitter.
8. If the batter crouches, pitch high and inside.
9. If the batter stands straight up, pitch him down.
10. If the batter steps in the bucket, pitch him low and outside.
11. If the batter lunges or overstrides, throw off-speed pitches or fastballs up and inside.
12. If the batter steps into the plate, pitch him fastballs up and inside.
13. If the batter displays nervousness or white knuckles, make him wait, then throw curves or change-ups. This tactic is effective in pressure situations.
14. If the batter has a flat (horizontal) bat, pitch down.
15. If the batter has a perpendicular (vertical) bat, pitch up.
16. If the batter holds his hands high, pitch up.
17. If the batter holds his hands low, pitch away.
18. If the batter uses an open stance, pitch him inside.
19. If the batter stands too close to the plate, pitch inside.
20. If the batter uses a closed stance, pitch him outside.
21. If a hitter crowds the plate, throw off-speed pitches.
22. If a hitter stands too deep in the box, use off-speed pitches.
23. Crouch hitters like low pitches so pitch them high.
24. Against lunge hitters use a change-up or high, tight fastballs.
25. Hitch hitters should be pitched fast and tight, although change-ups are often effective.

Developing a Plan

Pitchers who are alert and focused will be able to mentally formulate a plan for each batter. For example, pitchers should ask themselves the following questions.

- Where can I throw the fastball to get him out?
- Will the batter swing at the fastball up and in when behind in the count?

- Where does the hitter have power?
- Can he hit a breaking ball?
- Will he make adjustments?
- Can he run?
- Is he a good two-strike hitter?
- What type of hitter is he? Power, spray, or what?
- Will he bunt for a hit?

Keys to Successful Pitching

The following are some important keys for pitchers to consider.

1. Try to stay ahead of a hitter and challenge him.
2. Make hitters hit your pitch. Don't give in to the hitter, especially when behind in the count.
3. Know your best pitch on any given night and use it when in trouble.
4. Have confidence and determination.
5. Know your weakness and try to correct it.
6. Know the number of outs, the score, the number and location of base runners, and so on.
7. Know the importance of the outs and the runners on base (tying and winning run).
8. Know who is covering each base.
9. Know the speed of your infielders.
10. Never show your temper or fight umpires. They will only get even.
11. Keep control of yourself when teammates make errors behind you.
12. Throw the ball hard; don't aim it.
13. Be the boss when you are on the mound. Be determined and assertive.

Warming Up

A brief aerobic run followed by stretching are two of the most important things a pitcher can do before and after pitching. Hanging from an overhead bar is beneficial, but one must be careful not to do it excessively, to the point of hyperextending the shoulder tendons and ligaments.

During the warm-up a right-handed pitcher should throw low and away, whereas a left-handed pitcher should throw low and inside to a right-handed hitter. Using these targets forces the pitcher to use the proper follow-through to complete the motion. The catcher should help by giving the proper target.

The pitcher should strive to develop a groove during warm-up so that the ball lands in the same spot every time. The warm-up is a great time to think about not overstriding, a mistake that young pitchers commonly make when trying to overthrow.

Each pitch must be warmed up from both the windup and the stretch. Once the pitcher begins to feel loose, he can move back and warm up from an overdistance of about 100 feet and finish at 60 feet, 6 inches. He should then warm up slowly and from a shorter distance with the curveball to get the proper release point and rotation. He can move back to the mound to finish.

Preliminary actions of the pitcher, such as the windup stretches, have little relationship to the mechanics of throwing. These actions are commonly used to relieve stress, to build rhythm, and to create deception. But some or all these preliminary actions may give the pitcher an edge in the competition against the batter or runner. The pitcher should put on his pitching jacket after the warm-up and between innings, but he should never warm up with the jacket on his arm.

Cooling Down

Pitchers should stretch both before and after pitching. They should then cool down for 5 to 10 minutes by walking while wearing a jacket. They may place the throwing arm in ice water as far as the midarm and place a large cold pack over the shoulder for about 20 minutes.

A pitcher is only as good as his legs; therefore, he must do a great deal of running. Because more velocity comes from the lower body (52 percent) than from the arm (24 percent) and the wrist and hand (24 percent) combined, every pitcher should run daily. We suggest continuation of the preseason distance-running program mentioned in chapter 5.

Pitchers should have two sweatshirts so that they can change if necessary. Pitching in a T-shirt or no baseball undershirt at all invites disaster. After pitching, the player should shower, dress, and get some rest.

Pitch Counts and Overuse Injuries

Overuse is a common cause of arm injury. Because this type of injury is often preventable, high school and youth baseball leagues have rules and regulations specifying the number of innings pitched and the amount of rest needed in a given period. In 1995 USA Baseball conducted a survey to investigate what the relationship should be between the number of pitches thrown and the length of rest needed. Most baseball experts believe that the number of pitches thrown in one performance is a better method of determining the rest needed than the number of innings. In addition, a pitcher should be limited to two appearances a week, with consideration given to participation in multiple leagues, playing other positions, and practice.

Table 7.1 shows the maximum and minimum number of pitches that should require a specified rest.

Table 7.1	Maximum/Minimum Pitches Per Game Based On Age								
Pitcher's age	Maximum pitches/ Game	Day 1	Rest	Day 2	Rest	Day 3	Rest	Day 4	Rest
8 – 10	52 ± 15	21 ± 18		34 ± 16		43 ± 16		51 ± 19	
11 – 12	68 ± 18	27 ± 20		35 ± 20		55 ± 23		58 ± 18	
13 – 14	76 ± 16	30 ± 22		36 ± 21		56 ± 20		70 ± 20	
15 – 16	91 ± 16	25 ± 20		38 ± 23		62 ± 23		77 ± 20	
17 – 18	106 ± 16	27 ± 22		45 ± 25		62 ± 21		89 ± 22	

Getting the Signs

By rule the pitcher must take the catcher's signs on the rubber. He uses a relaxed stance so that the feet allow the body to be preturned to first base. A right-hander's feet should be opened to first base, and a left-hander's should be closed to first base. It is also preferred that the southpaw's pivot-foot heel be about one inch off the rubber. This position permits better movement with the feet when throwing to first base.

The pitcher should not always accept the first sign from the catcher, but neither should he take too long and risk putting the defense to sleep. He should occasionally shake off the catcher, especially in a sure fastball situation, using the head and glove for deception. In a sure fastball count when he wants to throw a breaking ball, he should have the catcher simply call for the breaking ball and not shake off any sign.

The pitcher must guard against establishing a pattern that the hitter can time. He must do something different—pump once or twice, walk around the mound, make the hitter wait—yet still work fast. Overdoing it may cause the fielders to lose concentration.

After accepting the sign and when going into delivery, the pitcher uses his body to hide the baseball. Two sets of signs should be used with runners on base. Signs must be changed on every pitch with a runner on second to prevent him from stealing the catcher's signs and relaying them to the hitter.

Set Position

The feet should be in a staggered position so that the heel of the front foot is in line with the toes of the pivot foot. The hands rest on or near the belt buckle in a relaxed position. The weight is on the back foot so that the pitcher can quickly pick up and put down the front foot without overstriding.

The pitcher always begins the delivery while looking toward home plate, never while looking at the runner. This is an important point. Pitchers will often be wild to the plate because they pick up the target too late. The pitcher can look to the base as many times as necessary to hold the runner, always making sure to pick up the target before making the pitch.

Holding Runners

Pitchers have the responsibility to stop the running game. In most cases the opponent's running game depends on exploiting the pitcher's inability to hold runners close to the base. The typical defensive strategy is to throw to first base two or three times in running situations. My rule is to throw early and often. If you believe you have thrown over enough, then you throw over again.

In total, the pitcher has five choices in holding runners close to bases— stepping off the rubber, holding the set, throwing to the base, using the slide step, and throwing the pitchout. By using all five choices, the runner will have difficulty analyzing the pitcher's motion to get a cue to run.

Time your pitchers to determine the motion time. Start the stopwatch with the initial hand movements and stop it at the point of release. Use the standard of 0.6 seconds as excellent, 0.8 seconds as average, and 0.9 seconds as poor. The pitcher must be able to make the base runner stop. Allowing a walking lead is an invitation to disaster.

After moving to the set position, the pitcher simply steps off the pitcher's rubber with the rear foot, quickly breaks the hands, and turn as if to throw to first. To prevent a balk call by the umpire, the step must be backward and without hesitation. The final position off the rubber should have the shoulders turned and the hands ready to throw.

When coming to set, the pitcher simply holds the ball for an extended period. He has no thought of pitching the ball. This action will freeze the runner. (Currently, many runners are taught to say "UCLA" as a timing technique. Some pitchers pause in the set position for a specific time, which allows the runner to time his break precisely.)

The pitcher must learn how to throw to bases within the preliminary motion. He must be able to throw on the way up, on the way down, and from the set position. To make a quicker throw, he should separate the hands before any foot or shoulder movement to the base. The hand should come up out of the glove rather than down. Quickness with the upper half of the body and accuracy, not velocity, is a crucial factor in all pickoff attempts. The throw should be low and to the inside, using a short arc for a quick release. The more dangerous the runner, the more the pitcher must throw to the base to keep him close.

If a right-handed pitcher has a predetermined intention to throw to first base, he should place his body weight on his left foot. This allows

a

him to move the feet more quickly. The throw should be a quick snap throw.

Left-handed pitchers must look the same from the set position to the primary balance position, then quickly put the foot down and use a snap throw.

The pitcher should develop a modified slide step. This is executed by quickly bringing the front knee back toward the rear knee, rather than lifting the front leg. We advocate this for all right-handed pitchers as the primary movement. Left-handers can also use the modified slide step as a variation to confuse a base runner, especially a runner on second base. In (a) the pitcher pushes hard on the pivot foot to prevent coming forward too soon. Photo (b) shows the front knee coming toward right knee without a high leg lift. Remember to maintain good front side mechanics (c).

Modified slide step.

b

c

Pitchers should also develop a slide-step delivery, but they should use it sparingly because it reduces velocity. A pitcher should use the pitchout only when he knows the runner is stealing. To prevent loss of velocity, the rear foot should be pressed as hard as possible into the ground. This allows for a well-balanced delivery with a good push off the rubber. The pitcher should avoid falling into a pattern that allows the runner to identify the logical pitch on which to steal.

Pickoff Move

The purposes of pickoff moves are to hold the runner close, keep the double play in order, and get an out. Most good pickoffs require quickness.

To make a good pickoff move, body weight should be on the back foot, a stance that will improve quickness. The pitcher has a good chance to pick off the runner as he is leading off, but he must try to throw over as the runner lifts his right foot. The standard jump turn with a short step and a short arm stroke is the quickest and normally the best move.

To pick off base stealers, all pitchers should learn a balk move, such as a step at 45 degrees and then a throw to first base, a quick pitch without setting the hands together, a forward-to-backward weight shift, or a hand fake and throw.

Right-handed pitchers should learn to throw to first using the technique with the heel down, a short-arm-action arc, and a quick six-inch step. Right-handed pitchers can also use the "Maryland move." As the pitcher stretches, his left foot moves to about 45 degrees rather than to the staggered position. From this open position, he throws to first base. Another good move for right-handers is to step off and pause one second, then throw to first base. In the photos on page 124 the pitcher takes the catcher's sign in a normal manner (a) then moves his front foot into the set position while stepping toward first base (b); as his hands reach a throwing position, he quickly throws to first base.

Any left-handed pitcher who allows a big lead or the advantageous break to the base runner is either grossly stupid or doesn't care enough or both. The left-handed pitcher must control the base runner.

For the left-handed pitcher the basic concept in developing a good move to first base is to maintain what he does mechanically during his natural motion to the plate. When throwing to first, he should duplicate what he does to the plate until the right leg gets to its highest point. The left-handed pitcher must learn to step beyond a 45-degree angle. He should set up his move by looking at home and throwing to home. After he has set up the runner, he should look, step at the 75-degree angle, and throw to first base.

He begins by setting the head and eyes at 45 degrees, using peripheral vision to see the runner. When throwing to home or first, he must consistently maintain the ankle and toe extension and flexion. When throwing to first, the toe always points toward first, no matter where the step lands. The front-side elbow and knee must work in unison.

Use progressive drills to develop a balk move. The pitcher should begin with a step directly to first, then 23 degrees, 45 degrees, and finally 68 degrees.

Another move for left-handers is the slow-motion, or hold, move. This move is effective when runners are taking too big a lead and are guessing. We also use it in first-and-third situations.

Another method is the quick step-off move and flip throw, which is effective against a one-way lead and against players trying to get a good jump in first-and-third situations. Pitchers should not show a slow move to first base because the runner may use a first-move step.

a

Maryland move.

b

c

A good balk move for southpaws is to pick up the front foot and put it back down in the same place with a quick flop throw. The first baseman's moves must be coordinated with the moves of both right-handed and left-handed pitchers.

Another method to confuse a runner's timing is to step off, turn, and break the hands. Or the pitcher can simply hold the ball and not step off until the batter calls time. Both of these actions seem to take the anticipation of a pitch from a runner.

Fielding the Position After the Pitch

When a pitcher releases the ball, he is no longer a pitcher but another infielder. He should be alert and ready to make all plays.

Infielding

The pitcher should anticipate what play he must make if the ball comes to him. Like any infielder he makes the play without being told. He should not have to wait for the catcher to call the play.

On all balls hit to his left the pitcher immediately breaks for the first-base bag. If necessary, he covers first base. If not, he keeps out of the play. The pitcher should field as many bunts as he can.

When runners are advancing and the play might be made at either third base or home plate, the pitcher runs halfway between them and prepares to back up the base. With this mental preparation, the pitcher must be ready to spring into action.

Bunts

In a possible bunt situation, the pitcher should throw the fastball shoulder high and hard. Depending on the chosen defense with men on first and second, and with a bunt in order, the pitcher covers the first-base side of the field and the first baseman must stay back (this is explained in detail in chapter 11). The pitcher breaks hard going in by shoving off the back leg and bouncing off the mound. He should be deliberate when fielding bunts.

The pitcher should make sure he sees the ball going into the glove before looking at the target. He plants the rear foot so that it is perpendicular to the line of the throw. He stays low when throwing, keeping the knees bent for power.

Balls bunted down the first-base line. The right-handed pitcher doesn't have time to straighten up. He should try to stay low and throw inside the diamond so that the first baseman gets a good picture of the ball. The pitcher may even have to throw underhand depending on the time involved and how close he is to the bag.

A left-handed pitcher must pivot to his right and do a half turn. He should be sure to have something on the throw and keep inside the diamond so that the throw will not hit the runner in back.

Balls bunted straight at the pitcher. The pitcher should field the ball in the glove and do first things first. He should take a short crow hop, set himself, throw with something on it, and show confidence in his arm.

Balls bunted down the third-base line. A right-handed pitcher goes to the right side, plants his right foot, and comes up throwing. The left-handed pitcher fields the ball in the glove, pivots to his right on a half turn in fielding the ball, and comes up throwing in two counts.

Fielding bunts and throwing to second base. The pitcher should know which infielder is covering a base and anticipate where to throw. He must have control of his body so that he doesn't throw off balance. On the ball bunted to the left, a right-handed pitcher will field the ball, plant the right foot and make a half pivot, open up the hips, and throw with something on the ball. On the ball bunted to the right, a right-handed pitcher will field the ball, do a complete pivot, and throw off the right leg with something on the throw.

On the ball bunted to the left, a left-handed pitcher will field the ball, do a half pivot, plant the left foot, and then throw the ball with something on it, all in one motion. On the ball bunted to the right, a left-handed pitcher will field the ball, plant the left leg, open up or pivot depending on where he fields the ball, and throw to second base with something on it.

Fielding bunts and throwing to third base. When fielding the ball to his right, a right-handed pitcher fields the ball and does a pivot to his left, opens the hips, plants the back foot, and throws to third base (a complete turn is usually necessary). When fielding the ball to his left, a right-handed pitcher does a complete turn, plants the back leg, and throws in a hurry. This is a difficult play that requires excellent athletic ability.

A left-handed pitcher, on a ball to his left, charges the line, fields the ball, does a half pivot, plants the foot, and throws. A left-handed pitcher, on a ball to his right, fields the ball, stays low, opens the hips, and may throw sidearm depending on where he fields the ball.

Covering First Base

On all ground balls to his left, the pitcher breaks hard and fast to cover first base, running directly toward the base.

He takes the throw about five feet from bag, staying inside and touching the bag with his right foot and turning in so that he can keep out of the runner's way. The pitcher should not snatch at the ball, should not fight it. He must be relaxed when fielding this tossed ball.

When the first baseman boots a ground ball, the pitcher goes to the bag in the same fashion. But when the ball is kicked, he should stay at the bag and not run by the base. He puts one foot on the bag and stretches out when necessary as a first baseman would.

After tagging the bag he turns toward the diamond so that runners won't step on or run into him. Also, should there be other base runners, he turns in to prepare himself for a throw to third or possibly home. He must be alert and prepared for the next play.

Throwing to Second Base for a Double Play

The pitcher should always know who is covering the bag so that he can correctly lead the infielders. Most of the time it will be the shortstop, because he is coming toward the bag. It is easier for the pitcher to throw to him and for him to execute the double play. Communication must occur before pitching. The pitcher should lead the throw to the shortstop. When the second baseman is covering the base, the pitcher should throw directly to him.

Rundown Play

When a runner is caught between bases, the pitcher should step back off the rubber and move directly at him. The goal is to make the runner commit himself before throwing. The pitcher must not run out of control; he may even walk. He goes to the base where there is only one infielder.

Covering Home Plate on Wild Pitches and Passed Balls

After a wild pitch or passed ball with a man on third, the pitcher should quickly come off the mound and run to home plate. He catches the throw, puts the glove on the front corner of home plate, and lifts with contact. He should never use the pitching hand or block the plate because an injury could occur.

Backing Up the Bases

The pitcher has the primary responsibility to back up throws to third base and home plate. When runners are advancing to third or possibly home, the pitcher must determine where the relay throws will go.

To help gain time, the pitcher runs halfway between third and home, simultaneously gaining depth. Once he determines where the play will be made, he backs up the base.

It is important to use the whole field. We prefer that the pitcher go all the way to the fence and face the field. If he faces the field, runners tend not to run on the throw. If the baseball goes past both the fielder and the pitcher backing up the base, the runner will run when he sees the pitcher turn his back to the field.

Lead-Up Drills

When teaching any aspect of pitching, lead-up drills are helpful. Progressive drills that break down the various parts are the preferred method. This method enables the pitcher to focus on a particular facet of pitching without the confusion related to such a complex athletic skill.

Learning a skill is significantly different from performing a skill; therefore, teaching requires different strategies, and the student's actions require different tempos. When doing any of the lead-up drills, the objective must be clearly defined to achieve the desired result.

When learning a skill is the object of instruction, movement should be slow and focused toward perfection. When learning to perform the skill, however, the exercise must be done at nearly full speed to simulate game situations. Performance tends to be extremely outcome oriented.

We use these progressive lead-up drills:

Quarterback Drill

Purpose: To locate the proper arm slot in the throwing motion

Implementation:
1. This drill is done with a partner.
2. At distance of about 45 feet, the pitcher kneels on one knee. The back knee is on the ground with the front foot closed.
3. Using good mechanics, partners play catch with emphasis on keeping the front shoulder closed.

Step-Ups to Primary Balance

Purpose: To develop rear leg strength and the primary balance position

Implementation:
1. The player begins by squarely facing the bench in the windup position.
2. Using the pivot foot he steps up onto the bench with the foot perpendicular to the direction of the target.
3. He visualizes an imaginary target 60 feet, 6 inches away.
4. He completes the step-up to the hand break at the apex of the knee lift, then maintains balance for one full second.
5. He steps down and repeats.

Secondary Balance Drill

Purpose: To teach pitchers the secondary balance position and to focus on keeping the weight back so that explosive hip rotation can occur later

Implementation:

1. The pitcher assumes the secondary balance position with the front elbow, nose, and front knee pointed directly at a target 60 feet, 6 inches away. The front foot is closed at about 45 degrees, and the baseball in the throwing hand is pointed away from the target. The head must be over the center of gravity, and the weight on the back leg.
2. From the secondary balance position the pitcher moves to the primary balance position and holds that balance for several seconds.
3. He returns to the secondary balance position and repeats.

Square-Up Drill

Purpose: To develop trunk rotation and hand speed

Implementation:

1. The pitcher squares the shoulders and feet to the target. This drill can be done with a partner or wall.
2. Without stepping or pivoting, he aims the front shoulder, extends the arm, and throws to finish with the proper follow-through.

Shift Weight and Rotate Late

Purpose: To teach timing of the trunk rotation and increase velocity of the throw

Implementation:

1. The pitcher assumes the secondary balance position with the front elbow, nose, and knee pointed at the target, which is 60 feet, 6 inches away. The front foot is closed, and the throwing arm is up and back with the baseball pointed away from the target.
2. From that position the pitcher shifts his weight back and forth several times.
3. Then, at the end of the forward motion, he rotates the trunk aggressively and throws the baseball.

Milk-Crate Drill

Purpose: To teach the pitcher to throw over the lead leg

Implementation:
1. With the pitcher in the set position, place a milk crate so that the pitcher must lift his rear leg over the crate when he throws.
2. Then have the pitcher throw to a catcher at 60 feet, 6 inches. In obtaining proper rear leg lift, he must not kick the crate.

Four-Corners Drill—Pitching

Purpose: To develop control in the strike zone

Implementation:
1. This drill can be done by throwing the pitch to a catcher or by using a target without throwing the ball.
2. Have the pitcher assume either a windup or set position.
3. Have the catcher show targets in the following sequences:

   - The right-handed pitcher throws three reps of three pitches down and away from the arm side and one pitch up and in. He then throws one set of three pitches down and away and one pitch up and away.
   - The left-handed pitcher throws two reps of three pitches down and away. He then throws two reps down and away and one up and away.

   Quality feedback is a vital tool in developing effective, consistent pitching. Use charts such as those on page 131 as tools to record the pitches and developments of a game.

   Pitching is the cornerstone of all championship baseball teams. By working fast the pitcher can help keep the concentration of the defensive players at a peak, resulting in less errors and more alert play. By throwing strikes and changing speeds the pitcher issues less walks, consistently pitches ahead in the count and keeps the batter off balance.

DATE: _____ OPPONENT: _____ SITE: _____

TIME: _____ SCORE: Arundel_____ Opp._____ WON-LOST: _____ KEPT BY: ____

No. B/Pos	NAME		NOTES

PITCHER	INN.	FB	CB	SLIP CH	SL	KN	TOTAL	R	H	BB	SO	FIRST PITCH S/T
	1											/
	2											/
	3											/
	4											/
	5											/
	6											/
	7											/
	8											/
	9											/
	10											/
	11											/
	12											/
	TOTALS											/

NOTES: _____

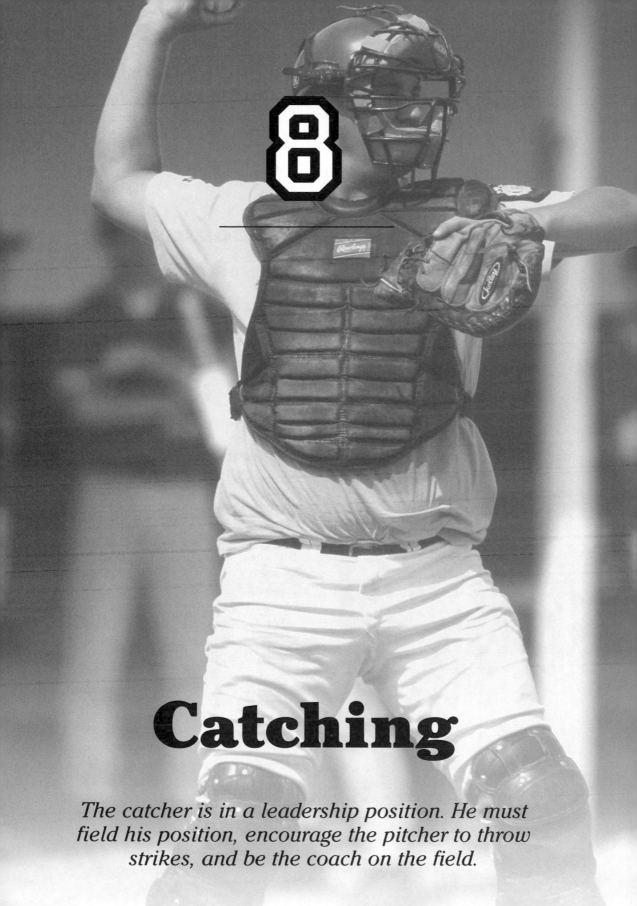

8

Catching

The catcher is in a leadership position. He must field his position, encourage the pitcher to throw strikes, and be the coach on the field.

Every good defensive ball club begins with an outstanding catcher. The catcher must be athletic, enthusiastic, mentally tough, intelligent, and possess good baseball tools. If he has any defensive weakness, the opponent will exploit it to advance extra bases. The catcher's arm strength alone will determine the aggressiveness of the opponent's base running game.

Leadership and Positioning

The catcher must be a leader, a take-charge guy. He must take control of the game by being assertive and full of hustle. His play sets an example for the rest of the team. It's his show, and he must run the ball club correctly. It takes guts and a good head to catch. Size, fast hands, and a strong throwing arm are some of the physical qualifications of a good catcher.

Signals to the Pitcher

One of the catcher's jobs is to be the right-hand man to the pitcher. The catcher must guide the pitchers into throwing strikes and reading the hitter. To do this, the catcher sends signals to the pitcher. The feet are shoulder-width apart, turned so that the catcher faces the shortstop. The right knee points at pitcher's shoulder with the fingers on the inseam and the glove on the knee to protect the signal from being seen by the third-base coach. The catcher should also be sure that the batter isn't watching the signal.

Catchers can use this simple and quick way to give signals to communicate with the pitcher:

- Five fingers or two fingers means a fastball.
- Four fingers or one finger is a curveball.
- Three fingers are for whatever other pitch the pitcher throws.

Fastball, five fingers.

Fastball, two fingers.

Curveball, four fingers.

Curveball, one finger.

Pitcher's choice, three fingers.

The catcher gives only one sign. If the pitcher shakes it off, the catcher gives another sign. The runner on second base will probably never quite decipher the signs and will be unable to pass along the pitch to the batter. With this system, the signs remain the same, whether there are runners on base or not. Because the signs never change in this system, less confusion should occur.

Stance

In the stance the catcher must stay low with the tail down, keeping the elbows outside the knees. The feet should be wider than the shoulders and flat footed with weight on the balls of the feet, toes pointed out, and the left leg and foot forward and in front of the right leg. The hips should be above the knees. The catching arm is out front and slightly flexed. The catcher uses a half target rather than a full glove target because showing the full glove locks the wrist. The bare hand should be held flat behind the glove with the thumb behind the index finger. The catcher puts pressure on the left foot because the right foot must move to throw. With weight on one foot, the player can shift. The closer together his feet, the quicker he can throw. The catcher looks like a jockey riding a thoroughbred horse in a Triple Crown race. Without runners on base the throwing hand is behind the arm-side leg so that foul balls are less likely to cause injury.

Catcher's stance.

Distance From the Hitter

A common problem is setting up too far from the hitter and home plate. This positioning causes the pitch to travel farther than necessary. The result is that the pitcher may lose some called strikes because the catcher receives the ball out of the strike zone.

To set up correctly, the catcher extends the arm so that the glove can almost touch the batter's elbow. When setting up, he splits home plate by moving the inside or outside foot to the middle of home plate. He shifts as late as possible to avoid tipping the pitch location to the hitter.

Visiting the Mound

A visit to the mound is occasionally required. Those visits must have a specific purpose—to discuss strategies for preventing stolen bases, to discuss strategies to use against the hitter, to restore a pitcher's concentration, to remind him of proper mechanics, to review signs, or to give the pitcher a brief rest during a long inning. The catcher should try not to visit the mound at the beginning of an inning because doing so stops the flow of the game. He should hustle to the mound and speak assertively. He is in charge!

Receiving the Pitch

The object is more than just catching the ball. We want to help the umpire call correctly every strike a pitcher throws and then some. Good catchers help the pitcher get strikes called. They don't cost him strikes because of poor receiving skill.

As the pitcher breaks his hands, the catcher relaxes his hands and makes a small half turn with the glove, as he would when holding a glass of water. This action allows him to frame the ball simply by folding the glove into the strike zone.

Positioning With a Runner on Base

The feet are spread wider than the shoulders and stay even with the left foot in front of the right foot. The weight is on the balls of the feet with most of the weight on the left foot so that the right foot can move quickly. The butt is low. The throwing hand is behind the glove, ready to make the exchange. To throw, the catcher uses either a jump turn or a jab step forward with the back foot.

Position with runner on base.

Pulling Pitches

Just catching the ball is not enough. How the catcher catches the pitch greatly affects the pitcher's performance and, therefore, the outcome of the game. The catcher must be sure to stay low in front of the umpire. In a nonrunning situation, it is critical to hold the close pitch. The catcher uses soft hands and turns the glove slowly as the pitcher throws the ball. As the catcher receives the pitch, he funnels (pulls the pitch) the glove and ball to his belly button. This goes for either inside or outside pitches.

Blocking Balls

Possibly the most important part of catching is blocking balls. All baseball players must learn to field ground balls, but the catcher may not need to catch the ball. He should block it. This play separates the players from the wannabes. Preventing base runners from advancing on passed balls and wild pitches is a critical defensive skill that demonstrates determination and desire to excel.

Blocking the ball in the dirt is called walling the ball. The catcher cuts the distance from the ball to himself and stays relaxed to block the ball as he goes to the knees. He places the hands with the thumbs out be-

Pulling pitches.

tween the legs and lets the shoulders roll forward to cup the ball. He should *block* the ball, not catch it. He must learn to surround the ball. He should anticipate the breaking ball in the dirt and compensate for it. The glove blocks the hole between the legs and protects the bare hands and wrist behind the glove. The catcher bends slightly forward at the waist and angles the body to deflect the ball to home plate. He follows the ball with the nose and eyes. Using the soft Incrediballs®-brand safety balls to block pitches is a safe method to teach and learn this skill.

Blocking the ball.

Throwing

Many professional scouts believe that throwing is the most important baseball tool for the elite catcher. The catcher must be able to throw accurately to second base in 2.0 seconds or less and to throw out 33 percent of runners attempting to steal. The throw is off the back foot with the knees bent and the arm extended, but a long follow-through is unnecessary. A grip across all four seams creates better carry on the thrown ball. The throw should stay up rather than sink. The catcher should use the short arc to bring the ball quickly up

Throwing position with runners on base.

out of the glove. He should always be ready to throw, always throw overhand, and always challenge the runner! A good habit to develop is to throw through the bag at the chest height of the infielder.

The key in all throwing is good footwork. Moving the rear foot to a position perpendicular to the line of the throw is the universal technique for all throwing. Using a carioca step with the inside pitch to a right-handed hitter is often helpful.

If the pickoff opportunity presents itself, the catcher should be mentally aggressive by throwing behind the runner. This is one of the most exciting plays in baseball, and the catcher should use it! When throwing to third base, he must divide home plate into thirds. If the pitch is on the inside or middle of the plate, he steps behind to throw. If the pitch is on the outside, he steps close to the foul line to throw in front of the batter.

Fielding Bunts

The bunt is the catcher's ground ball. He should react quickly like one of the great cats and pounce on it. Some catchers react like the lethargic cartoon cat Garfield and wait for someone else to make the play.

On bunts in front of the plate and down the first-base line, the catcher should approach the ball low and take it with two hands. He then plants the right foot firmly and throws in a sidearm motion to first base. On throws to second or third base, he throws overhand. It may be necessary to take a step or two toward the infield grass to clear a path to avoid the runner.

When fielding bunts along the third-base side, the catcher approaches the ball on the field side with his back to the pitcher. He then bends over with two hands, takes the ball into the mitt with the right foot firmly planted, and throws overhand to first base. Catchers should have these attitudes and abilities:

- Be active defensively.
- Keep runners close to bases by attempting pickoff plays. Good catchers have no fear of throwing to bases.
- Field ground balls in front of home plate by scooping with two hands and staying low to throw quickly.
- Try to catch all pop-ups with both palms up.
- Be able to change signs to the pitcher with runners on base.
- Signal first the type of pitch, then give the location of the pitch.
- Never allow the pitcher beyond a 2-2 count. The catcher should have the pitcher throw the best pitch that he is throwing that day. Sometimes pitchers have better command of a particular pitch on a certain day.

- Stay low with the glove extended to receive but with the elbow flexed.
- If the umpire blows the pitch, communicate the fact to the pitcher and coaching staff by tapping the mask.
- Know the hitter's weak points.

Catching Pop Flies

To catch a pop fly, the catcher turns his back to home plate. He holds on to the mask until he locates the ball, then throws it away from the pop fly, staying under control and moving toward the ball. He catches it directly over his head with the fingers up, when possible. This method allows a second chance if the ball hits the heel of the mitt. The catcher should remember that pop flies will curve back to him. He must be careful not to run over the ball, proceeding carefully, even "creeping," after it.

Pickoff Plays

There are several strategies for catchers to use in pickoff plays.

1. When throwing to third base, if the pitch is outside, the catcher should use the jab step and throw in front of the right-handed hitter.
2. When throwing to third base, if the pitch is down the middle or inside the catcher should use the drop step and throw behind the right-handed hitter.
3. When throwing to first base, the catcher should not move his feet but pivot the left knee toward first base to close the shoulder and then throw from the knees.

Tennis-Ball Drill

Purpose: To develop soft hands for receiving the pitch

Implementation:
1. A catcher in full equipment sets up to receive a pitch without wearing the mitt.
2. The coach throws pitches to the catcher, who catches with one hand.
3. The coach can vary velocity and location of the throw.

Shadow Drill for Catchers

Purpose: To teach the various stances and movements of the catcher

Implementation:
1. Have two catchers face each other and assume a catching stance.
2. One catcher is the leader, and the other must mirror the movements. Those movements should include taking his stance, throwing, blocking pitches, and catching various pitches. The tempo varies from slow in the beginning to faster to when learning to compete.

Scramble

Purpose: To teach catchers to block pitches, recover, and make the next play

Implementation:
1. Have infielders cover their respective bases and have the catcher wearing full equipment behind home plate.
2. The coach has a bag of baseballs about 30 feet from home plate on the infield.
3. The coach defines a situation for the catcher, for example, a runner on second base. (This is important because the catcher must anticipate where the next play will be.)
4. The coach throws a pitch in the dirt for the catcher to block. After blocking the pitch the catcher must quickly get to his feet, retrieve the baseball, and throw to a base.

Fielding Bunts

Purpose: To teach the skill of fielding bunts

Implementation:
1. All catchers line up behind home plate, each in full gear.
2. The coach stands in either batting box with a baseball.
3. Infielders, including a pitcher, take their positions on the infield.

4. Have the pitcher throw a pitch. As the ball passes the plate, the coach rolls a ball down either base line or in the middle of the field about 15 feet from home plate.
5. The catcher fields the bunt using the appropriate technique.

Tag Play at the Plate

Purpose: To learn proper technique for catching throws from the outfield

Implementation:
1. The catcher wearing full equipment stands at home plate in position to block the plate.
2. All the other players on the team stand just into the outfield, each with a baseball in hand.
3. Beginning at the left each player throws a ball on one bounce to the catcher.
4. The catcher makes the catch, drops to block the plate, spins to tag the imaginary runner, then recovers and looks for the next play.
5. Repeat the sequence by moving clockwise around the outfield, giving everyone a chance to throw to the plate.

Down-the-Line Throwing

Purpose: To develop accuracy by reducing movement of the thrown baseball

Implementation:
1. Catchers work in pairs. They begin by standing about 60 feet apart, then work back to about 130 feet.
2. They remain stationary and play catch down the line. They should attempt to make the ball rotate from twelve o'clock to six o'clock so that little or no movement occurs on the throw.

Four-Corners Drill—Catching

Purpose: To teach the footwork needed to throw to the various bases

Implementation:

1. Position a catcher at each of the four bases.
2. They throw the ball around in the following pattern. The first throw is across the diamond. If the player receives the ball from across the field, he throws right to simulate a throw to first base. If the player receives the ball from the left, he throws across to simulate the throw to second base. Eight throws will complete one round.

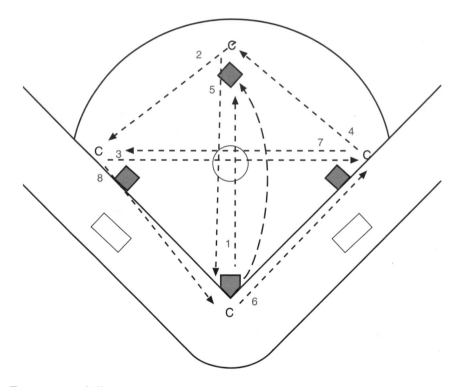

Four-corners drill.

Quarter Eagles

Purpose: To develop biomechanics and cardiovascular fitness

Implementation:

1. Select one catcher as the leader.
2. The other catchers line up facing the leader so that they can see him well enough to follow him.
3. The leader begins hopping in place, then makes quarter turns either clockwise or counterclockwise. The others try to follow the leader. The leader should not turn in such a way that the others cannot see him.

Plays at the Plate

On close plays at home plate, the catcher should take the throw on the third-base side in front of the plate so that he can more easily block the runner from scoring while tagging him out. He can use either the tag with two hands (punch) or the one-handed scoop tag.

Punch tag.

Scoop tag with one hand.

If the throw to the plate is late and he has no chance of making the tag in time, the catcher should leave the plate and try to prevent another runner from advancing.

The catcher is in the ultimate leadership position. Because of his position on the field, he is in full view of all the action. His discipline, enthusiasm, knowledge, and communication skills are key assets to success. Catchers must field their own positions, encourage pitchers to throw strikes, and be the coach on the field. Catchers play a critical role in the success or failure of any baseball club.

9

Infielding

Expect that every ball hit will be hit to you.

ood infielders want the ball to be hit to them. They know the number of outs, the inning, the count, and the score. All plays are made based on the situation, so they know it!

Position in the Infield

Four primary base positions are included in the infield: first baseman, second baseman, third baseman, and shortstop. Each player should find his position with everyone bunching to the middle of the field. They then adjust from there, depending on the scouting report or game observations. Starting positions on the field are 72 feet off the line for the shortstop and second baseman, 24 feet off the line for the third baseman, and 22 feet off the line for the first baseman.

Infielders should play no deeper than the location from which they can throw out the runner at first base on all routine plays. They should also try to avoid playing the one-hop distance off the infield grass. This is no-man's land, a playing depth that leads to many errors. They should play either on the grass or at a two-hop depth, if the infield is up.

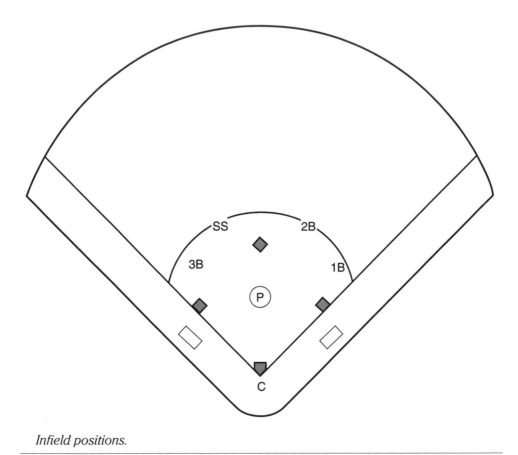

Infield positions.

Correct athletic position.

Ready Position

Rhythm at the starting position puts the body in motion. To get started, infielders use the tennislike "gigglefeet" technique. They get into position to catch the ball by moving the feet.

Athletic Position

The athletic position is a narrow stance with the weight on the balls of the feet and the center of gravity relatively high. From that stance the player can move quickly in any direction. His eyes should be looking into the hitting zone, not at the baseball. His knees are bent, and the glove is open. When the ball is hit, he gets a quick jump on the ball and moves like a sprinter.

Throwing

The prerequisites to being a good infielder are having insight into the action and a strong throwing arm. Every practice and game begins with proper warm-up and throwing. Players should always use correct fundamentals in throwing practice, especially footwork. Accurate, powerful throwing is a result of good balance. Because most infielders are right-handed, they most often throw off the right foot. To make accurate throws, players should get the right foot planted perpendicularly to the target. They always throw to a spot or target with

Incorrect athletic position.

a fine focus. Maintaining a curved posture and keeping the knees bent allows players to use the power of the legs and hips. They attempt to catch with two hands so that they can use the short arc to take the ball out of the glove quickly. When taking the ball out of the glove, the fingers are set across all four seams, with fingers apart at eleven o'clock and one o'clock. A good baseball habit is to throw over the top. Players should learn to use quick feet, such as a jump turn to get rid of the ball quickly.

Players must never hold back on a throw. Nobody is perfect, so players need not be afraid to commit an error. If a player is going to make an error, he may as well make it a good one. He should throw it out of the stadium, if he can. The result is the same—two bases.

Infielders finish warming up by throwing extended distances to strengthen the arm. They should avoid warming up with knuckleballs and curves; they are not pitchers! A tough habit for infielders to break is curving the fingers of the glove. We have found it better to use a flat glove folder inside out.

Throwing grip.

Fielding

Fielding is an individual skill in a team setting. Each infielder must throw accurately, tag out base runners, consistently catch ground balls and pop flies, and use this knowledge to coordinate a solid team defense with the other members of his team.

Ground Balls

In order to be consistent in fielding ground balls, the infielder should get into the athletic position and never raise up from it. To have soft hands, he keeps the hands extended out front while moving. The glove is always in front so that he never loses sight of it. The back stays flat. The player moves so that the left foot and glove hit the ground together. He gets as low as the ground ball by bending the knees and hiding behind the glove.

The infielder should consider using the funnel technique. He lays the glove open and keeps it open as he moves to the ball. By bending the knees he can see the ball better when he catches it. As he catches the ball, he pulls or funnels it into his belly button. When fielding ground balls he always tries to catch the big hop or the short hop rather than the in-between hop. Players must never loaf on ground balls because the tendency is to try to make up for time by rushing the throw. Remember to move through the ball. He must never be at a dead stop when fielding a routine ground ball. The last two steps are important: The infielder charges slowly-hit ground balls, and prepares to throw sidearm. He stays down, not straightening up to throw, and continues to run in a straight line. He avoids changing direction toward the base, which would create footwork problems. The glove hand should not move backward when playing short hops. If it does, the ball has more time to bound upward, increasing the chance that a short hop will become an in-between hop. The infielder should always try for hard-hit line drives because the ball may have topspin that causes it to sink into his glove.

Fielding ground balls.

Pop Flies

On pop flies the infielder drop steps and, if necessary, turns clockwise to put the glove over the proper shoulder and sprints to a spot deeper than where he expects it to land. Fly balls should be caught above the shoulder if possible. The infielder should call for the pop fly, go back for it until he hears from the outfielder, and then get out of the way.

Covering the Bases and Tagging the Runner

To apply the tag, the infielder straddles the bag, has the ball in the glove with the glove closed tightly, and tags with the back of the glove. On a close play he takes the glove down and up quickly. The umpire should see that the infielder knows the runner was out, but the player should leave the glove on a sliding runner because the runner may come off the base. A play that may occasionally work is to fake the runner by standing straight up with the hands at the sides as if there will be no play. The runner might slow down and allow himself to be tagged out. This play has the best chance to work at third base or second base when the ball is behind the runner.

First Base

The importance of the first baseman primarily revolves around the ability to consistently catch the baseball. Not only is he expected to handle normal throws, but he is also expected to be the savior on bad throws. First basemen are required to make quick decisions during bunt and cutoff plays. As a fielder, his importance is equal to that of a power hitter.

Tagging the runner.

First basemen should use these guidelines for playing their position.

1. With no man on first base, the first baseman plays at least 12 to 15 feet behind the base and 22 feet off the foul line. He plays close enough to the bag that he can arrive on time to be a target for his infielders. He must never be late to the bag! He then gets in athletic position to receive the throw. The closer the infield gets, the lower he gets; therefore, he only needs to move up.

2. He straddles the bag to shift the feet, sliding the feet along the bag. On the ball to the right, the left foot moves to the right corner of the bag and the player stretches with the right foot. On the ball to the left, the right foot moves to the left corner of the bag and the player stretches with the left foot.

3. To receive low throws, the first baseman catches with the fingers up when possible. To catch high throws, he stands on the top of the bag to be taller. He uses the two-handed technique of catching when possible. When stretching for a throw, he lands on the front heel, not the toe. He should practice this often, especially when the other infielders are practicing throws to first. The first baseman should work on tagging the runner coming to first on throws up the line. On the tag play from a pitcher's pickoff attempt, he catches the ball, drops to the right knee, and slaps the glove to the far corner of first base.

4. The first baseman should learn to break off the base to a fielding position when holding a man on first. The break must be toward second base rather than home plate. This deeper position puts the first baseman in a better position to execute the pickoff play successfully with the catcher.

5. When holding a base runner at first base, the left-handed first baseman breaks to the depth position after the pitch. He cannot reach normal depth. This is the only time that the first baseman ends up in no-man's land. When the pitcher throws to first base on a pickoff attempt, the first baseman squares up with the pitcher, shows an inside target, catches the throw, and drops to the right knee as he slaps the tag on the runner in a downward motion. The right-handed first baseman plays with the left foot toward the pitcher. In the Palmeiro technique, the first baseman plays off the base toward the pitcher. Then, just before the pitcher's delivery, he moves back toward the base to force the runner to shorten his lead. This jab-step technique must be coordinated with the pitcher's move and often requires a signal between the pitcher and first baseman.

6. The first baseman should check to see that the batter-runner touches all four bases, including first base, as he turns.

Make the tag and be alert for the next play.

Second Base

The second baseman is an important player in in the total scheme of team defense. Arm strength is crucial because of the long and difficult throws that must be consistently made. Quickness of feet, arms, and hands are essential components to play second base. The second baseman is also involved in more double plays than any other infielder.

Second basemen should use these guidelines in playing their position.

1. When tagging the runner in the base path for the double play, the second baseman tags the runner with both hands. The baseball is in the throwing hand, and the gloved hand provides protection.

2. If the runner stops, the second baseman runs him back to first base far enough to permit a rundown before throwing to first to retire the batter. Then the infielders get the runner out in a rundown to complete the double play.

3. The second baseman should understand that the runner cannot leave the base line.

4. The second baseman should establish the range of the first baseman and run him off most ground balls hit between them. He can increase his reach by taking a deep path to ground balls by going into short right field to catch the ball.

5. He should check to see that all runners touch second base when they turn.

Third Base

The third baseman plays the hot corner. Because he often plays at a shallow depth, the third baseman must react quickly on both hard hit and slowly batted balls. His reactions both physically and mentally must be without hesitation.

Third basemen should use these guidelines in playing their position.

1. Regular depth is 12 to 15 feet behind third base and 24 feet off the foul line.

2. The infield-up position is in the baseline and 24 feet off the foul line.

3. Double-play depth is 12 feet from the baseline and 24 feet off the foul line. This is on the edge of no-man's land. The third baseman should play either up or back but never in no-man's land.

4. The third baseman doesn't hold the runner on third base. He allows the pickoff plays to put the runner at risk.

5. The third baseman attempts to field all ground balls to his left. He is in a better position to make the play than the shortstop, especially on force plays at second base.

6. On a sacrifice-fly situation, he checks to see whether the runner left the bag early.

7. He checks to see that all runners touch the bag when they turn at third base.

Shortstop

Leadership qualities are important because the shortstop is the captain of the infield. These qualities include functional intelligence, instinctive intuition, and stable emotional self-control. Shortstops should use these guidelines in playing their position.

1. On ground balls to the extreme right, we recommend a slide rather than a dive for the ball. When perfectly executed, the player winds up with his right foot braced against the loose dirt piled up by the sliding foot.

2. The shortstop must not loaf on any ground ball and then try to make up lost time by firing the ball.

3. He must vocally keep the other infielders mentally alert and alive.

4. The shortstop has the primary responsibility to prevent the steal of third, so he must hold runners close.

5. He should check to see that all runners touch second when they round the base.

Following are drills for infielders.

Instructional Sequence for Ground Balls

Purpose: To teach the proper techniques for fielding ground balls

Implementation:
1. Infielders assume the athletic position and then move to field the ball.
2. **No-ball fielding.** Place several infielders in a line side by side about 6 feet apart. On command by the coach, each infielder rehearses fielding an imaginary ground ball. It best to do this slowly at first and then gradually speed up the movement. Continue doing this until the players master the skill.
3. **Stationary-ball fielding.** Place several infielders in a line side by side about 6 feet apart. Place a baseball about 10 feet in front of each infielder. On command by the coach, each infielder moves forward and into position to field the stationary ball.

4. **Fielding rolling ground balls.** Place the infielders in two single-file lines of three players. The infielder in the front of one line begins the drill by rolling a baseball to the first player in the other line. He then rotates to the back of his line. The other infielder fields the rolling baseball, rolls the ball back to the player now in front of the first line, and rotates to the back of his line. This pattern creates a continuous exchange of fielding rolling balls.

5. **Fielding bouncing ground balls.** Place the infielders in two single-file lines of three players. The infielder in the front of one line begins the drill by throwing a bouncing ground ball to the first player in the opposite line. He then rotates to the back of his line. The other infielder fields the bouncing ball, throws a bouncing ground ball to the player now in the front of the first line, and rotates to the back of his line. This pattern creates a continuous exchange of fielding bouncing ground balls.

Fielding Fungoes

Purpose: To develop the skill to field various ground balls

Implementation:
1. The infielder takes his position. The coach should be near home plate with a fungo bat and a baseball.
2. The coach hits a ground ball to the infielder, who fields the ball and makes a predetermined throw to either first base or second base. He completes the play by making a throw.
3. The coach varies the drill by changing the speed of the batted ball from slow to hard hit. He also varies the drill by hitting the ball to either the left or right of the infielder. The coach should attempt to create gamelike situations with this drill.
4. To make the drill even more gamelike, the coach can hit fungoes from the first-base side to the third baseman or the second baseman. Or he can hit fungoes from the third-base side to the shortstop or the first baseman.
5. For efficiency, use two fungo hitters, one hitting from each side of home plate.
6. Modify this into a double-play drill by using only one fungo hitter.

Double Plays

All ground balls with a runner on first are not possible double-play balls. The velocity of the batted ball and the speed of the batter-runner are the determinants. To set up for the double play, the middle infielders move to double-play depth, two steps directly toward home plate and three steps nearer to second base. We call this two by three.

The key is to get there early, break down, get under control, work behind the bag, and expect a bad feed! As the middle infielder approaches the base, both hands are together with the fingers up. The middle man should always receive the ball with both hands.

The fielder is the "sure man." The pivot is the "quick man." The feeds by the second baseman are either underhand, baseline play, the pivot, 180-degree turn. All feeds should be chest high. The feeds by the shortstop are underhand, regular, the rise, and backhand. The underhand feed is used when moving toward the second baseman's right. After catching the ground ball, he tosses the ball underhanded to the shortstop. He then veers toward center fielder to clear the path of the shortstop turning the double play.

The baseline play is used on a ground ball either in the baseline or on the infield grass. The second baseman flips the ball to the shortstop by leading with the elbow and using a backhanded toss with the thumb down.

The pivot is squaring up to catch the ground ball then simply making a quarter turn of the body without moving the feet, then throwing the ball overhand to the shortstop. Some coaches teach moving the feet to throw, however, I prefer to have them drop their center of gravity and turn.

The 180 is used on a ground ball to the second baseman's left (glove side), after catching the baseball he continues to turn to his left until he is in position to throw overhanded to the shortstop.

Footwork by the second baseman begins with the left foot on the bag. As he receives the ball, he either steps back, steps across, or moves for an inside bad feed to hop and cheat toward third base. Footwork for the shortstop entails using short steps without covering ground. The shortstop must distinguish between the ground ball that he must catch and throw to the second baseman from the one that he can field and follow with a tag of the bag and a throw to first. The Cal Ripken unassisted play, stepping on second base with the left foot while throwing to first, is the best way to execute the double play without throwing.

Second basemen often catch ground balls near the base path and must tag the runner. When tagging the runner, he should use both hands, holding the ball in the throwing hand and using the glove for protection. He should not chase the runner because the runner cannot run out of the base line. If the runner stops, the second baseman runs him far enough back to first base to permit a rundown before throwing to first to get the batter. The infielders then get the runner in a rundown to complete the double play. Following is a goal drill for double plays and an offensive performance chart to record individual performance.

Five-Foot-Circle Double-Play Drill

Purpose: To teach double-play techniques for middle infielders

Implementation:

1. Draw a 5-foot circle around second base. Place a safety screen about 45 feet down the line toward first base. When the double play is turned, the infielder must stay inside the circle. Observing this rule eliminates excess movement and emphasizes the quickness necessary for executing the double play.

2. Put several players in a line at shortstop and second base. Be sure they begin at the proper depth and distance from the base.

3. The coach kneels behind the pitcher's mound and about 40 feet from second base. From there he rolls a ground ball to either the shortstop or the second baseman.

4. The infielder fields the ground ball and delivers the ball to the other infielder using the appropriate technique.

5. The second infielder receives the throw and, while staying in the 5-foot circle, quickly throws to the safety screen.

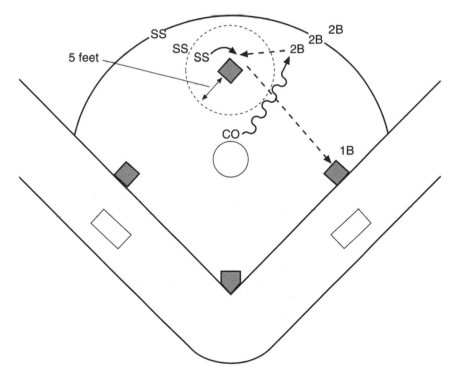

Five-foot-circle double-play drill.

Your Team Name Here

Offensive Performance Chart

Key: + = succeeds, — = fails

Player	Signs	Sac bunt	Pinch hit	Advance runner	RBI w/ 2 out	RBI from 3B	Steal	Base-running	Special

All infielders must expect that every ball will be hit to them. By knowing every aspect of your responsibilities and anticipating the possibilities through a valid analysis, you can adapt quickly to accommodate the circumstances. If you hesitate, you may lose.

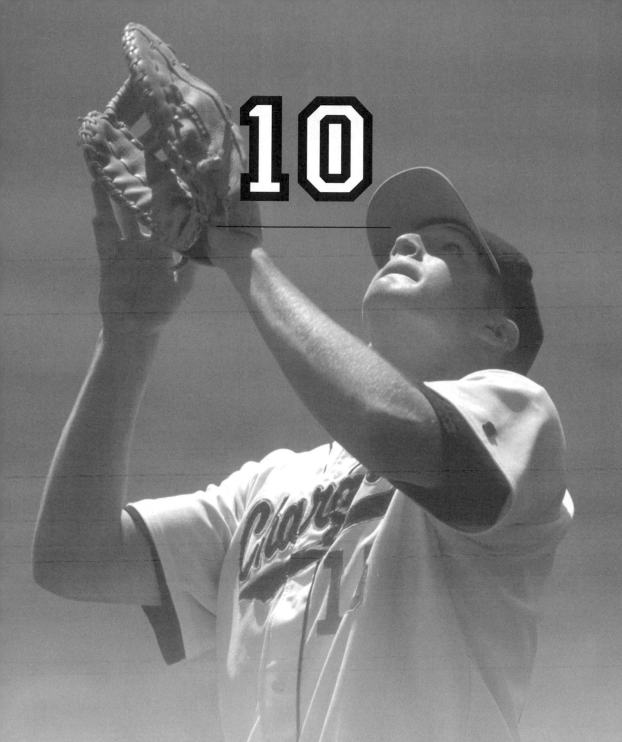

10

Outfielding

Play your best and your best will be enough.

s soon as an outfielder gets on the field, he must determine how the ball bounces off the wall and how the ball meets the corner of the fence. He must also look for changes in wind and sun, which will mean learning to use sunglasses when necessary.

During the game, he should say to himself, "Every ball is going to be hit to me." By preparing mentally before every pitch he will always be prepared. He should assume that nobody else will make the play and expect the worst so that he will be ready.

Being alert to special situations means knowing when the bunt is in order, knowing when the tying or winning run is at bat or on base, knowing who has exceptional speed. Outfielders should study the hitters to know who pulls and who hits with power, and play accordingly.

Position in the Outfield

Positioning of the outfield as a unit is essential to the overall success of the team. To establish the depth of all three outfielders, we begin at 280 feet. From there adjust relative to the hitter's power by moving either in or out by seven steps (20 feet). This places the outfielder at either 260, 280, or 300 feet from home plate.

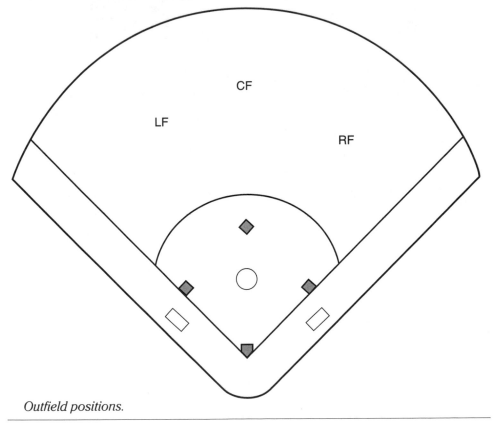

Outfield positions.

In order to establish positions that will effectively cover the outfield, locate relative to the foul lines. Both the left and right fielders should be 90 feet from the foul lines. The center fielder is two steps off a direct line from dead center field. From that position, the outfielders as a unit adjust three steps in the direction of the hitter's tendencies. By careful observation and analyzation, you can learn whether a particular hitter has tendencies to show a slight pull or hit to the opposite field. If the hitter is a dead pull or late hitter, move three more steps. As a rule, move 10 to 20 feet in either direction of the ball.

Ready Position

The ready position consists of a narrow stance, with the weight on the balls of the feet and the center of gravity relatively high so that the outfielder can move quickly in any direction. He should walk into the ready position.

The outfielder should use all his senses. His eyes read every pitch, inside and outside. By reading the bat angle, he will know where the ball is going. His ears can pick up the sound of the bat hitting the ball, which will tell him how far the ball is going.

Many baseball coaches neglect outfielders during batting practice, which is unfortunate because batting practice offers the best opportunity to learn outfield play. Shagging off the bat daily during live batting practice will greatly improve an outfielder's defensive skills.

Throwing

The key to being a good outfielder is knowing the action and reacting with a solid throw to throw out the base runner. Here are some tips that outfielders should use to make good throws.

- Always grip across all four seams with your fingers apart.
- Always throw overhand with full arm extension.
- Use the high-knee crow hop to target and create momentum and power.
- Tuck your glove against your chest when throwing to prevent flying open.
- Be sure that you finish with the chest over the front foot.
- Overemphasize the follow-through when warming up and during infield practice. This will strengthen your arm and make it more accurate.
- Always hit your cutoff man to prevent further advance by the runners.

- Don't worry about where the runners are. Just hit the cutoff man. Aim to hit the cutoff man in your head.
- Never throw through, that is, short hop, your infielders.
- With the baseball stops at the fence, step over the ball and then crow hop and throw.
- With baseballs on the glove side, run hard to cut off the ball. After you catch the ball, step and make a full turn to throw back to the infielder.
- After the catch, get the meat hand into the glove quickly.

Throwing Rules

Purpose: To know where to throw by reacting to the batted ball

1. If the ball is hit directly to you, throw out the lead runner.
2. If the ball is hit a few steps to your side and you are moving in as you catch it, look to the lead runner or throw to second base.
3. If you field the ball going away, throw to second base.
4. If the ball goes past you, throw to the cutoff man.

In some cases, throwing to second base is an excellent play because it keeps the double play in order.

Fielding

Outfielders should have speed and the ability necessary to get the jump on a batted ball. Often outfielders must wait patiently for that one play. However, they must be ready every pitch of the game because they never know which action will involve them. By properly charging ground balls, backing up infielders, making accurate throws, and catching fly balls, he can prevent the opponent from scoring runs.

Fly Balls

The first response in fielding a fly ball is to jerk the head back using the inner ear. These guidelines will help outfielders learn to field fly balls.

1. On fly balls over his head, the outfielder should use the drop step and then the crossover step. He should drop directly toward the straight-line route to the baseball.

2. Outfielders should always run full speed after fly balls, getting under them and waiting to make the catch. They should never glide to the

ball or get in the habit of timing the catch. They should avoid running with an extended arm. Instead, at the last second, they should stab the ball.

3. The outfielder should always stand deeper than where he thinks the ball will land so that he is able to turn through the ball when he makes the catch. If possible, he catches the ball going toward the infield. He should time the catch and go into a throwing motion. When possible, he should set up 6 to 10 feet behind the fly ball.

4. The outfielder should not get under the ball! Instead, he should keep the ball to the side.

5. The player should look the ball into the glove.

Get under a fly ball to make the catch.

6. On diving catches, the outfielder should use the shoulder-roll finish and get the glove up.

7. On sliding catches, he should use a pop-up slide with the glove to the side.

8. The outfielder should remember that the ball will always curve toward the foul line.

9. Most outfielders use a very large glove.

10. The catch should be made on the throwing side above the shoulder with both hands as the rear foot hits the ground.

Ground Balls

The key to fielding ground balls is to break hard on every play. Outfielders should charge all ground balls, even those hit directly to an infielder that appear to be sure outs. Outfielders should be in the habit of backing up their infielders. As an aside, with the no-play technique, the outfielder blocks ground balls on the right or left knee.

Infield Technique

The outfielder always fields the ball in front of himself. Right-handers practice fielding ground balls on the left foot. The outfielder charges at full speed until he is ready to make the catch, then crow hops to get under control. After catching the ball off the lead foot, he throws by planting the back foot. The outfielder should stare down low line drives and ground balls.

All-or-None Technique

This play is used only when the game is on the line. Outfielders charge the ground ball as hard as possible and then catch the ball on the glove side on the outside of the leg. Because this play must be made at full speed, it is dangerously susceptible to an error.

Mass Drill

Purpose: To rehearse the proper technique of fielding a fly ball and making a throw to throw out a base runner

Implementation:
1. Group all the outfielders, keeping about six feet between players in all directions. The players should face the coach.

2. The coach faces the group and gives the following oral directions. The outfielders move as a group by following the coach's directions.

The coach says, "Ready."	The outfielders assume the ready position.
The coach says, "Go back."	The outfielders move back four steps.
The coach says, "Move in."	The outfielders move in.
The coach says, "Catch the ball."	The outfielders simulate catching a fly.
The coach says, "High-knee crow hop."	The outfielders do a high-knee crow hop.
The coach says, "Throw."	The outfielders simulate a throw home.
The coach says, "Three hops."	The outfielders hop three times over the front foot.

Z Drill

Purpose: To learn to change direction while tracking a fly ball

Implementation:
1. Place an outfielder about 30 feet in front of a coach in the ready position.
2. The coach has three baseballs in his nonthrowing hand. He begins the drill by pointing in a direction.
3. The outfielder runs in that direction. The coach throws a fly ball so that the outfielder can catch it on the run. The player then quickly changes direction without losing sight of the coach. The coach throws a second ball in that direction so that the outfielder can catch it on the run. He again quickly changes direction without losing sight of the coach. The coach throws the third ball in that direction so that the outfielder can catch it.

ESPN Catch of the Day

Purpose: To learn how to play fly balls near the fence

Implementation:
1. You will need a Jugs® pitching machine for this drill. Place the machine near home plate. Adjust it to throw fly balls near the outfield

fence. Be sure to adjust the controls to make the ball curve toward the foul line.

2. Put one outfielder in the ready position about 15 feet from the fence, then shoot a fly ball toward the fence.

3. The outfielder moves to catch the baseball. Because of wind and the inconsistency of the machine, fly balls will vary from routine flys to drives that give the outfielder a chance to leap at the fence and take away a home run. Have fun!

Machine Fly Balls

Purpose: To learn to catch a variety of fly balls

Implementation:

1. You will need a Jugs® pitching machine for this drill. Place the outfielders in a line. Have one outfielder move into position apart from the others.

2. Put the pitching machine near home plate and shoot a fly ball toward the outfielder.

3. Change the drill often by changing the direction and velocity of the machine shooting the balls.

Consider these variations:

- Shoot line drives directly at the outfielder.
- Curve fly balls toward the outfielder. (Be sure that the ball curves toward the foul line.)
- Curve fly balls away from the outfielder (curve balls toward the foul line).
- Shoot fly balls out of the sun. (Have outfielders use helmets for safety.)
- Shoot low line drives or short fly balls that require the outfielder to make a shoestring catch.

An outstanding outfielder can be the most valuable property to the ball team. Just like the power hitter or power pitcher, outfielders contribute to the ultimate result of the game. To perform like a champion you must be ready to play your best and then your best will be good enough.

11

Team Defense

The importance of defensive execution is emphasized by the statistic that 40 percent of runs are scored in only 5 percent of the innings.

laying good defense requires teamwork—the ability to work together toward a common goal, to direct individual accomplishment toward organization objectives. Teamwork is the fuel that allows average players to attain excellent results. To win consistently, we must work harder on defensive strategy than we do on offensive baseball. All championship teams begin to win on defense. Such teams have the ability to play together. Games are often decided by the ability or inability to execute defensively.

One-Throw Rundown

The rundown is the most fundamental team play in baseball. Nearly every other defensive play can result in a rundown situation. We like to keep this play simple. When players recognize the rundown situation, the infielder must step to the inside of the baseline and run at the runner very hard. The pitcher goes to the base that has only one player.

As the runner nears the base, the receiver steps off and demands the throw. The gap should be closed so suddenly that the runner cannot stop or change direction. This play is made without speaking.

Defenses to Stop the Sacrifice Bunt

The keys to defending against the sacrifice bunt are to use two hands and to anticipate getting the lead runner. Several strategies are available to stop the sacrifice bunt in various situations.

1. The pitcher waits. If the first man in the inning reaches first base, the pitcher is required to throw to first. All teammates are looking to see whether the hitter shows the bunt.

2. With a man on first, use a standard rotation to the left with both the first baseman and third baseman charging. If the third baseman fields the bunt, the catcher covers third.

3. With men on first and second, use either "Larry" (left) or "Roger" (right) rotations. In either rotation the infielders are preset in the same locations with the first baseman up about 70 feet from home plate. The second baseman is three steps closer to home plate and two steps closer to first base. The shortstop moves into a position to hold the runner on second base. The third baseman is two large steps in front of the base line directly toward home plate.

- The Larry rotation is a standard rotation to the left. After taking the set position, the pitcher throws the ball to the plate and the

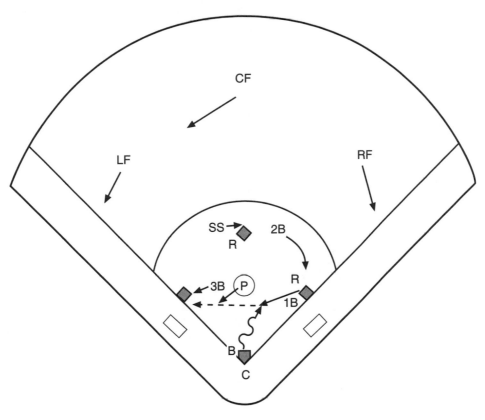

Larry rotation to the left.

batter shows bunt. The pitcher covers the third-base side, and the first baseman covers the right side of the infield. The second baseman covers first base, and the shortstop covers second.

The third baseman has a difficult decision to make. If the ball is fielded by the pitcher or first baseman, he covers third base. But if the ball is bunted hard and gets past the pitcher, the third baseman fields the ball and throws to first base.

With a runner on second, or runners at first and second, the third baseman must recognize whether the catcher can handle the bunt or whether he should him play it himself. If the pitcher fields the bunt, the third baseman must retreat to the bag for the throw. He takes a look at the bag and hustles but does not feel for it with his feet.

If the ball is bunted past the pitcher, the third baseman must field the bunt. Because the ball is often bunted hard, he should evaluate the possibility of a force play at second. If the force there is not possible, he should get the out at first.

- The Roger rotation is a rotation to the right, also known as the wheel play. From the preset position, after the pitcher throws to

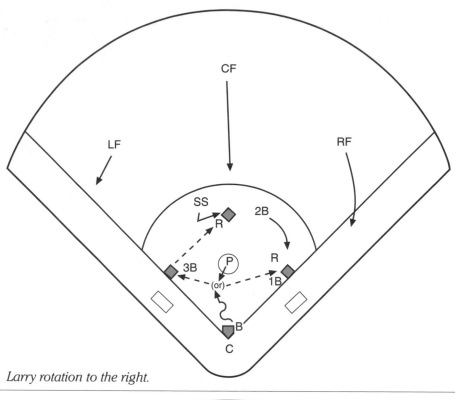

Larry rotation to the right.

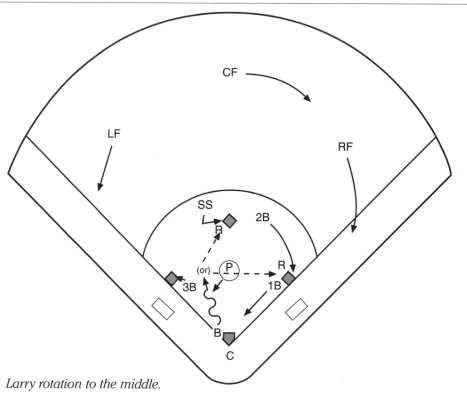

Larry rotation to the middle.

home plate and the batter shows bunt, the first baseman covers first base, the second baseman covers second, the shortstop covers third, the third baseman changes to field the bunt, and the pitcher covers the middle and left side of the infield.

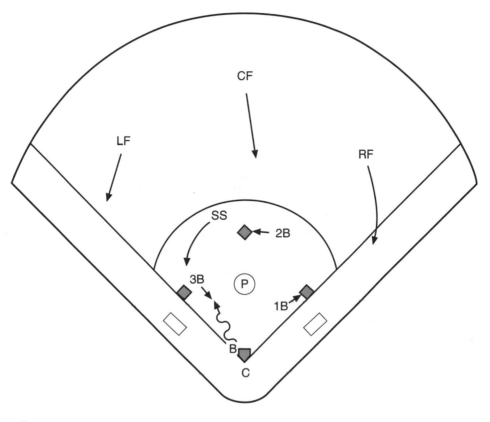

Roger rotation.

4. With men on first and second, the defense can use the charge play as shown on page 174, running a pickoff from the Roger (right) or Larry (left) rotations with the second baseman covering second.

5. Trapping the ball can be effective when the bunt is popped up. The pitcher allows the ball to hit the ground. We want him to try to field the bunt on a short hop to freeze the runner. Then, he always throws to the lead runner's base to get the force out.

6. The best defense against the suicide squeeze is to use pitchouts to deter the opposition from attempting the play.

7. On the five-man infield we move the left fielder to third base to hold the runner on third. He uses the same technique as the first baseman does. The other infielders play up to cut off the run.

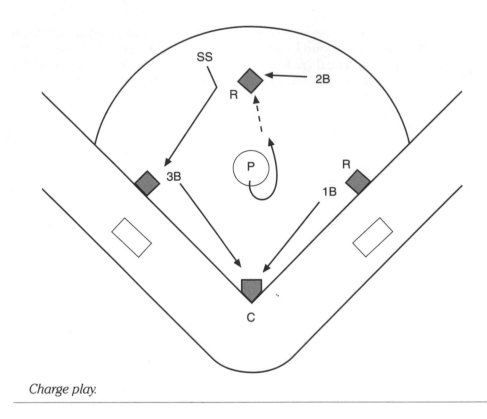

Charge play.

Pickoff Plays

The purpose of the pickoff play is to shorten the lead. If you get an out, it's a bonus! To determine which play to use, carefully observe the opponent and take whatever the offense gives. The runner's actions will indicate which play to execute. The runner can make one of four basic mistakes. He may take too large a lead, begin his secondary lead too soon, take an excessive secondary lead, or simply be lackadaisical and vulnerable.

When the primary lead is too large, we use the 50 series. If the secondary lead occurs too early, we have the pitcher turn from the secondary balance position in the 30 series play, also called the special series. If the secondary lead is too large, we use the catcher throwing or the 20 series. When the instant opportunity presents itself, we use the 10 series, or daylight, plays. If the situational strategy calls for the runner to be held close to the base, try anything! Most often that situation is when the runner is the winning or tying run.

We do not alter our positioning on the field to execute a pickoff play. The infield may be at double-play depth, in a bunt defense, or up on the infield grass. Some teams must align in a certain way to run a play, permitting an alert offensive team to anticipate the play. That isn't acceptable.

To solve that problem, we use a numbering system based on four basic conceptual series—the 10, 20, 30, and 50 series plays. The goal is to communicate the entire play simply and quickly. The 60 series, the hidden-ball trick, is fun to practice and sometimes works. The 99 play and the second-and-third defense play are special plays designed for specific circumstances.

The first number indicates the series and techniques to be used. The second number indicates the infielder who is involved—1 for the first baseman, 2 for the second baseman, 3 for the shortstop, and 4 for the third baseman. So, for example, series play 21 means that a play will be made with the catcher and first baseman; series play 34 means that a play will be made with a special pitcher and the third baseman. For example:

50 series is the basic multipurpose team play—51, 52, 53, 54

30 series is a play with a special pitcher and an infielder—31, 32, 33, 34

20 series is a play with the catcher and an infielder—21, 22, 23, 24

Teen series are daylight plays, plays of instant opportunity

60 series is the hidden-ball trick play—61, 62, 63, 64

99 play

Second-and-third defense play

50 Series

The 50 series pickoff play is our fundamental system of pickoff plays. Some people consider these timing plays. This is a play with many faces—one play fits all. Neither the location of the baserunners (which bases are occupied) nor the positioning of the infielders matters. We can run this series from any location.

The infielder may move any direction, except toward the base; therefore, infielders can play back, play up, set up for the bunt, play at double-play depth, or be moving away from the base. Once the infielder moves toward the base, however, the play will commence.

Executing the 50 Series Play

1. The infielder initiates the play by signaling the catcher.

2. The catcher's role is to answer the infielder and signal the pitcher that a pickoff will occur, not a pitch.

3. The pitcher's job is to set, check the lead runner, and wheel and throw when the catcher flashes his hand, which occurs when the infielder breaks.

- The windup position requires the pitcher to stay off to avoid a balk.

- From the stretch position, we prefer to use the 30 series in two situations. For a right-handed pitcher, we do not use the 54 pickoff play. And for left-handed pitchers, we do not use the 51 pickoff play. We prefer the 34 and 31 pickoff plays, when facing the infielder.

- Integration with the sacrifice-bunt defense is simple.
- The middle infielders can play the in-and-out game. The infielder not involved in the pickoff moves in and out to set up the pickoff play.
- Players can exchange positions and still know what to do, eliminating extra teaching time.

30 Series

We use the 30 series to combat the early secondary lead. This series can only be used when the pitcher is in the set position. The pitcher gives a signal to an infielder, such as wiping his hand on his pant leg. The infielder answers with a similar sign. The pitcher assumes the set position, looks at the runner, and then picks up his leg as if to pitch. When the infielder sees the sole of the pitcher's shoe, he immediately breaks to the bag. From the primary balance position, the pitcher throws to the infielder. Obviously, this series cannot be used by a right-handed pitcher going to first base or a left-handed pitcher throwing to third base. Those moves would be balks.

20 Series

The 20 series should be used with the runner who takes an excessive lead after the pitch. The catcher gives a sign to the infielder, such as picking up some dirt and tossing it at him. The infielder answers with a similar sign. After the pitch, the infielder immediately breaks to the bag and the catcher throws the ball to him.

When throwing to the third baseman, the catcher must avoid throwing through the runner. The throw to the first baseman must be very quick. The catcher can increase his speed by dropping to his right knee.

Teen Series

The teen series is also known as the daylight play. Some teams use only the shortstop, but I recommend using all the infielders. This play does not use any predetermined signs. As the pitcher moves to the set position, he looks at the infielder and the base runner. The infielder starts the play by placing space between himself and the runner. The infielder shows his glove to the pitcher and quickly moves toward the base. The pitcher uses his judgment. The best time to throw a wheel is when "daylight" appears between the infielder and the runner.

If the infielder breaks to the base and the pitcher decides not to throw, the pitcher must wait for the infielder to return to his position or step off the rubber.

60 Series

The 60 series is a theatrical play. It involves the entire team, including the players on the bench and in the bullpen. Anyone can indicate the play with a verbal sign. The pitcher can be in either the windup or the set position. After the pitcher assumes his pitching stance, he turns rapidly and makes a full arm and body fake as if he had thrown the ball hard but away from the fielder. In one fast motion he hides the ball under his armpit. The infielder dives for the errant throw, the outfielders chase and search for the phantom ball, and everyone screams "Run!" to create confusion and chaos. All the while, the pitcher is walking directly toward the base runner, hoping to catch him off base so that he can be tagged out. Players in the bullpen react as if the ball came in their direction and move to avoid the wild throw. This play requires a lot of choreography, but it is entertaining.

99 Play

With the infield up and a runner on third, the third baseman sprints towards home plate, hoping to bring the runner with him. The pitcher must pitch out to protect the infielders. Immediately at the start of the pitch, the shortstop breaks for third base and the catcher throws the ball to him in fair territory.

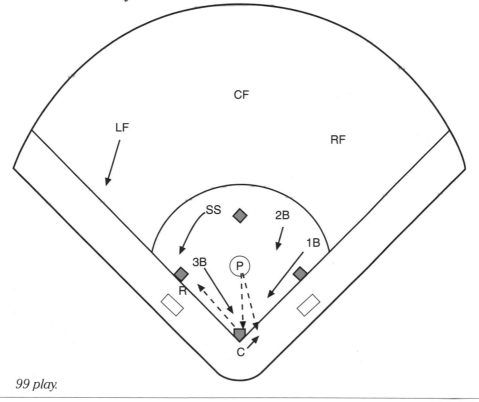

99 play.

Second-and-Third Defense Play

We use a special pickoff with runners on second and third because the runner at second base often feels extreme liberty to take a large secondary lead. The pitcher fakes to third with a full arm fake and then turns to throw to second, hoping that the runner there is not alert. Ordinarily, the second baseman covers the base on this pickoff. Again, the pitcher must be a good actor.

First-and-Third Defense

A few basic concepts govern first-and-third situations.

* The catcher must always look at the third baseman and check the runner.
* The pitcher should flag down (deek) or check all throws from the catcher. This deek should freeze the runner at third.
* The throw must automatically go to third if the third baseman raises both hands signaling that he wants the ball.
* Outfielders must back up bases.
* The middle infielder who is not covering the base must play the batter until the pitch is caught by the catcher; he must not back up second base too soon.

The defensive package of play choices includes several options.

* The catcher throws high and hard back to the pitcher
* The catcher throws to second base with three predetermined options for the infielders:

   1. Get an out and concede the run.
   2. Close up the left shoulder to catch the ball and throw home, not giving up the run.
   3. Concede nothing and use the home or tag play. "Bingo" is one oral signal to turn to make the catch and immediately throw home, and "tag" means to tag out the runner at second base.

* The catcher can make a full-arm fake throw to second and quickly throw to third. "Ham it, damn it" is one coaching cue. This fake must be full speed and convincing.
* Waggle. The pitcher from the set executes a fake to third and a quick turn to first base with readiness for a throw to first base. As the pitcher fakes to third, the third baseman breaks to the bag to help sell the play to the runners. The first baseman takes two steps off before the pitcher

initiates the play and returns to the base to catch the throw and tag the runner.

• The high school play is to tell the runner, "It's a foul ball." This is verbal obstruction and should not be used. We have included it because some teams still use this play. Your offensive team should know better than to be fooled by this unsporting act.

• The pitcher throws to third, and the third baseman throws to second. This play can be useful if your catcher cannot throw out runners.

• The pitcher steps off and fakes to second, then looks at third for a possible play.

• In the reverse waggle, the pitcher steps off the rubber, fakes a throw to first, and then quickly throws to third for a possible play.

Communication is important to a good defense.

Defense Against the Force Balk

The term *force balk* describes an early break by the runner on first base in a first-and-third situation. Our favorite defensive play is the Dodger D. To execute this play, the pitcher steps off the rubber and makes a good fake to third to make the runner dive back to the base. He then throws to second. If the runner doesn't return to third, the pitcher picks him off. The shortstop goes to second base, and the second baseman moves about 15 feet short of second base and looks for a throw from the pitcher. During the rundown infielders must make a good arm fake to force the forward runner to run home.

Wild-Pitch and Passed-Ball Defense

On a ball that gets by the catcher with a runner at third, the catcher retrieves the baseball, the pitcher covers home plate, and the first baseman backs up the pitcher in case of an errant throw. The direction the ball goes after getting by the catcher will determine the backup position for the first baseman. The catcher will often use a figure-4 slide (i.e., sliding like a baserunner then popping up for the throw) to get to the baseball.

Calling Fly Balls

Our goal is to catch all fly balls. Conflict sometimes occurs when more than one player can make the play. All fielders should move together toward the ball like dancers in a ballet. When a player gets close to the ball he should call for it. He must not call too soon. Once he decides to call for the ball, he uses his voice with authority.

Fly-Ball Protocol

With fly balls there is a certain protocol to follow: If two or more players call for the fly ball, the center fielder has priority over everyone; outfielders have priority over infielders; the shortstop and second baseman have priority over the first and third basemen; the catcher has priority over the pitcher, but the pitcher should catch any ball if he isn't called off; if a runner is stealing, infielders should fake the fielding of a ground ball (deek); the pitcher is the referee when two or more infielders are calling for the ball.

A special situation arises on a foul fly behind the plate with runners on first and third. The second baseman goes to the mound while the pitcher goes to the plate. After the catcher catches the foul pop-up, he should throw the ball to the second baseman to prevent the runners from tagging up and advancing.

Pitchout or Slide Step

Pitchout technique requires special coordinated practice time with pitchers and catchers. The team must have a simple pitchout signal. The catcher sets up as he would for an outside pitch. On the pitch he sets out at a 45-degree angle toward the pitcher and squares his rear foot with the direction of his throw. He gives the pitcher a chest-high target as he steps.

Intentional passes to hitters also require coordinated practices with pitchers and catchers. We prefer that the catcher stand erect with both feet together on the outside line of the catcher's box with his outside hand extended as a target. As the pitcher begins to throw, the catcher steps out and catches the ball in a position to throw. He may have an opportunity to pick off a relaxed runner.

The slide step is characterized by a very low knee lift to prevent the steal of bases. This technique should be used sparingly because all pitches thrown with it lose velocity. (Many teams have the coach call this technique from the bench rather than leaving to the players.) To reduce the loss of speed, the pitcher must keep his weight back and avoid shifting his weight forward too soon. We teach the pitcher to push down as he starts the slide-step delivery.

Backups, Cutoffs, and Relays

The purpose of cutoff and relay plays is to throw out the lead runner; if that cannot be done, the goal is to prevent other runners from advancing. Players must know the purpose if they are to learn to play these situations well.

We define the relay play as occurring after a ball is hit down the lines or up the alleys and past the outfielders. This ball is a sure double or more. The infielder is expected to throw out the runner. Cutoff plays are normally plays in front of an outfielder in which his throw would go directly to a base to throw out a runner. The key to the relay play is to make two good throws.

- The positioning of the infielder is 30 feet from the base on cutoffs. We do not want to cut good throws.
- Infielders move 30 feet into the outfield grass on relays, being sure not to drift deeper into the outfield.
- The outfielder makes the long throw, and the infielder makes the short, accurate throw.

- When the shortstop or second baseman is the cutoff man, he lines up to the plate or third base. He should "glide and decide."
- The oral cue for the relay man is "Hit me . . . hit me . . . hit me." The communication vocabulary for the trailer is "Let it go" or "Cut 1 (2, 3, or 4)."
- The outfielder's target changes depending on whether the play is a cutoff or relay.
- On cutoffs the outfielder aims for the knees. The low throw will stall runners from advancing on the throw.
- On relays the outfielder aims for the head of the infielder. The relay throw should not bounce.

The following cutoff plays are standard in most organizations. Unless the throwing arms on your club force a change, follow these cutoff procedures.

Situation 1—Nobody on Base, Single to the Outfield

1. *Ball to left field.* The shortstop lines up the throw. The second baseman moves to second base. The outfielder gives the shortstop a

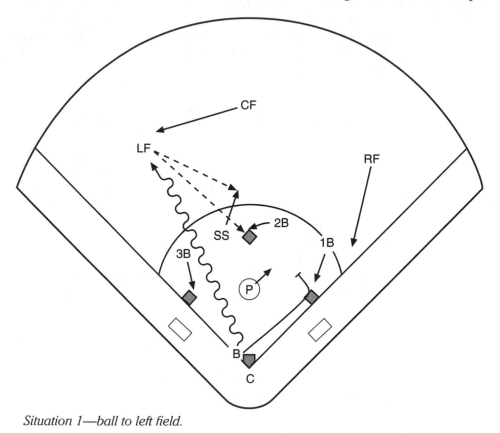

Situation 1—ball to left field.

nice, firm throw. On balls hit between the shortstop and third baseman when both make an effort for the ball, the third baseman will switch with the shortstop and take the cutoff position. If the ball is shallow into left field, we want the throw to come to second base in the air.

2. *Ball to center field.* The shortstop and second baseman orally communicate on this play. One will go out for the cutoff, and the other will go to second base.

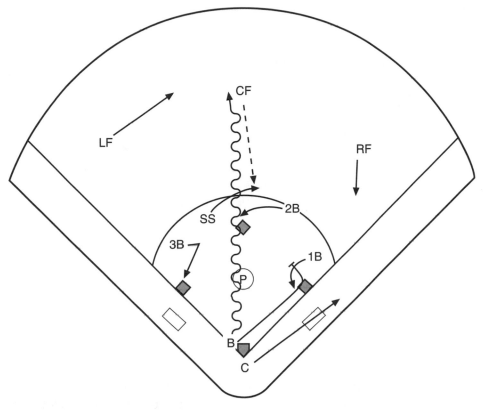

Situation 1—ball to center field.

3. *Ball to right field.* The second baseman lines up the throw. The shortstop goes to second base. The outfielder gives second baseman a nice, firm throw. On balls hit between the first baseman and second baseman when both make an effort for the ball, the first baseman will switch with the second baseman and take the cutoff position. The second baseman will go to first base. The catcher should go out and meet the ball for a possible play at third base.

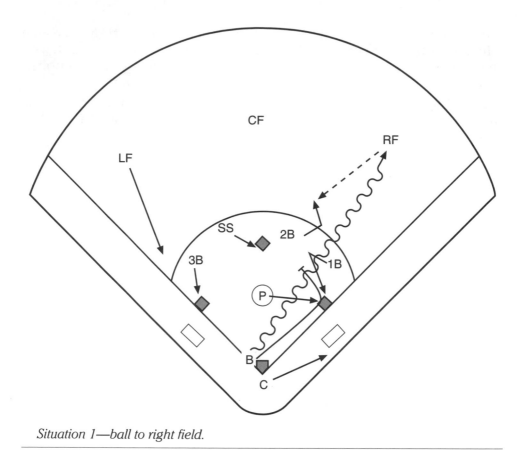

Situation 1—ball to right field.

Situation 2—Man on First, Single to the Outfield

1. *Ball to left field*. The third baseman goes to third base. The short-stop lines up the throw to third base. The second baseman goes to second base, and the first baseman goes to first base. On ground balls hit between the third baseman and shortstop when both make an effort for the ball, it is easier and more practical to switch duties. To do so, the shortstop goes to third base and the third baseman lines up the throw. The pitcher backs up third base in line with the throw.

2. *Ball to center field*. Assignments are same as on the ball hit to left, except the shortstop lines up the throw from center field to third base. The shortstop and second baseman should switch duties on the ball through the middle when both make an effort it. The second baseman lines up the throw and the shortstop goes to second base. The pitcher backs up third base in line with the throw.

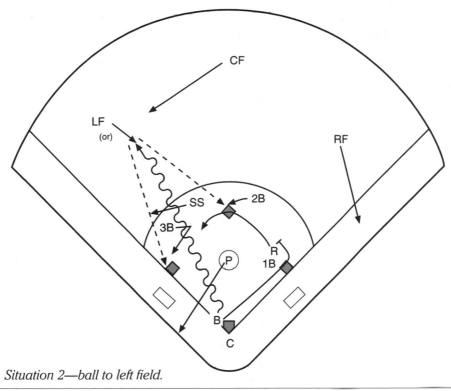

Situation 2—ball to left field.

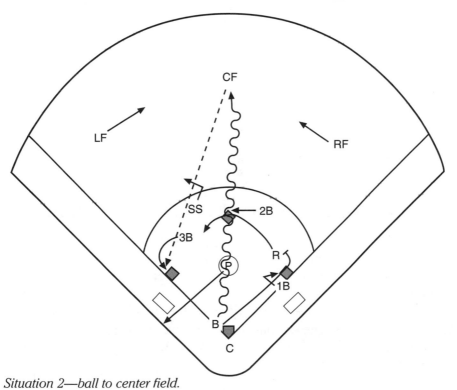

Situation 2—ball to center field.

3. *Ball to right field*. Assignments are same as on the ball hit to left, except the shortstop lines up the throw from right field to third base. On balls hit between the first baseman and second baseman when both make an effort for it, they should switch duties. The second baseman goes to first base, and the first baseman goes to second base. The pitcher backs up third base in line with the throw.

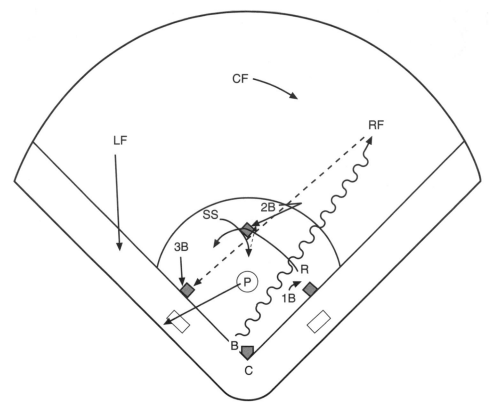

Situation 2—ball to right field.

Situation 3—Man on Second, Single to the Outfield

1. *Ball to left field*. The third baseman moves to cutoff position at the plate. The shortstop moves to third base. The second baseman covers second base, and the first baseman covers first base. The pitcher backs up home plate.

2. *Ball to center field or right field*. The first baseman moves to cutoff position at the plate, the second baseman goes to first base, the shortstop goes to second base, and the third baseman goes to third base. The pitcher backs up home.

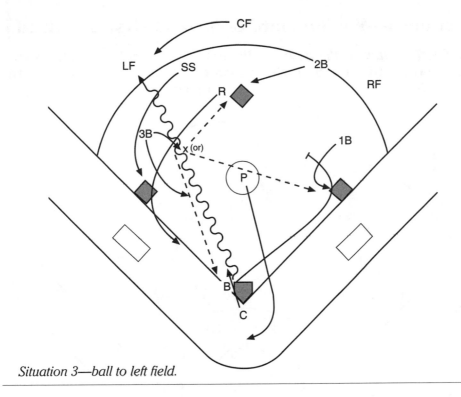

Situation 3—ball to left field.

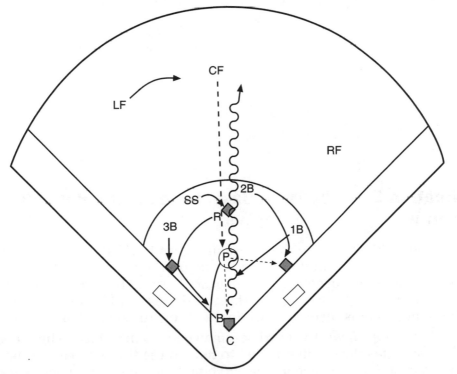

Situation 3—ball to center or right field.

Situation 4—Man on Third or Men on First and Third

1. *Sacrifice flies to the outfield.* Players take the cutoff positions that they used for the situation with a man on second and a single to the outfield (situation 3). The pitcher backs up home.

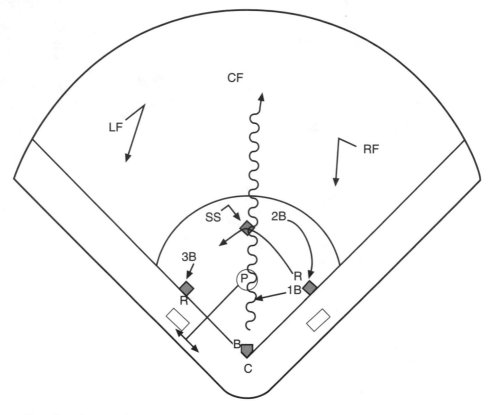

Situation 4—sacrifice flies to the outfield.

Situation 5—Nobody on Base, Long Single, Possible Double

1. *Ball to left field.* The third baseman goes to third base. The shortstop moves to the cutoff position to line up the throw to second base. The second baseman covers second base. The first baseman covers first base but is ready to back up the throw if there is a play at second base. The right fielder is ready to back up the throw to second base.

2. *Ball to right field.* The third baseman goes to third base. The second baseman takes the cutoff position to line up the throw to second base. The shortstop covers second base. The pitcher and left fielder drift toward the shortstop position to back up a possible play at second base.

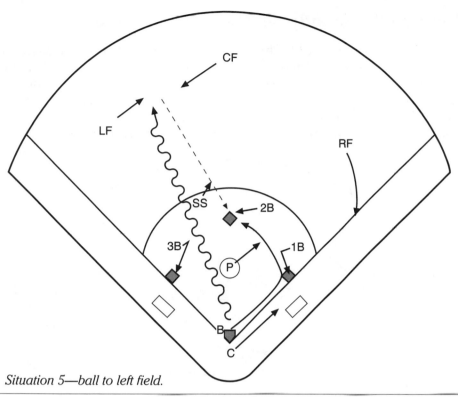

Situation 5—ball to left field.

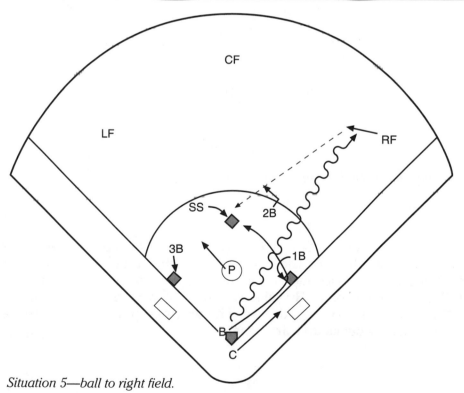

Situation 5—ball to right field.

Situation 6—Nobody on Base, Sure Double

1. *Ball to left-center field.* The third baseman goes to third base. The shortstop lines up the throw for a possible relay play at third. The second baseman trails the shortstop in a tandem as a safety valve and calls the play for the second baseman—"No play," "Third base," or "Second base." The first baseman trails the runner to second base for a possible pickoff from the relay man. The pitcher backs up third base.

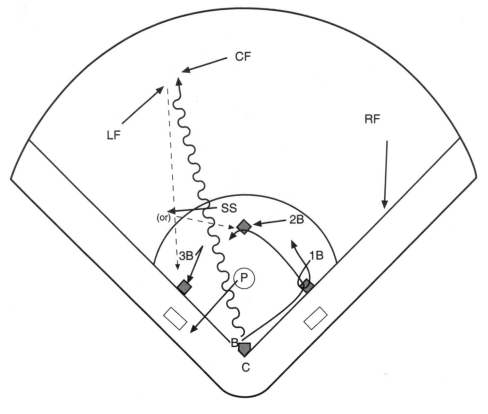

Situation 6—ball to left-center field.

2. *Ball to right-center field.* The third baseman goes to third base. The second baseman lines up the throw for a possible relay play at third. The shortstop trails the second baseman as a safety valve and calls the play for the second baseman. He yells "No play," "3" for a throw to third base, or "2" for a throw to second base. The first baseman trails the runner, and the pitcher backs up third base.

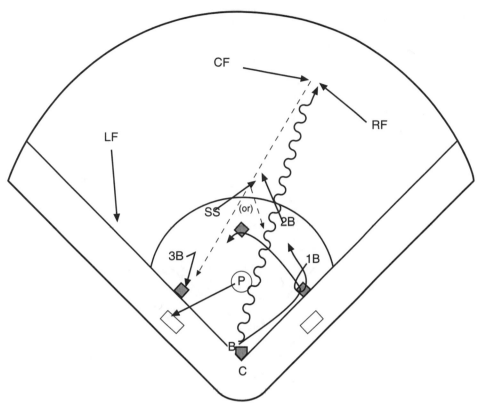

Situation 6—ball to right-center field.

3. *Ball to left-field corner.* The third baseman goes to third base. The shortstop moves to the left-field line in relay position for a play at third base. The second baseman moves to the bag and, as the sure double develops, drifts toward the shortstop position to retrieve a possible loose ball. The first baseman trails the runner to second base. The pitcher backs up third base in line with the throw.

4. *Ball to right-field corner.* The third baseman goes to third base. The shortstop goes to second base and, as the sure double develops, drifts into cutoff position for possible play at third base. The second baseman and first baseman move to relay position for a possible play at third base, with the best arm taking the relay position. The pitcher backs up third base.

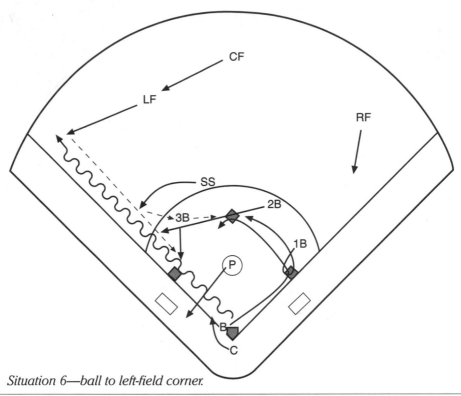

Situation 6—ball to left-field corner.

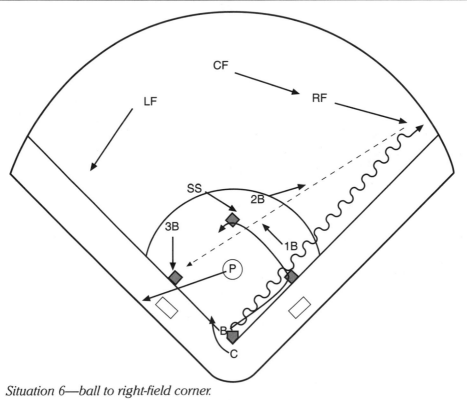

Situation 6—ball to right-field corner.

Situation 7—Man on First Base, Sure Double

1. *Ball to left-center field.* The third baseman goes to third base. The shortstop lines up the play for a possible relay play at home. The second baseman trails the shortstop as a safety valve and calls the play by yelling "Home," "Third base," or "No play." The first baseman moves to a cutoff position around the mound. The pitcher backs up home; if there is no play there, he backs up third base for a possible play. The right fielder is alert to cover second base.

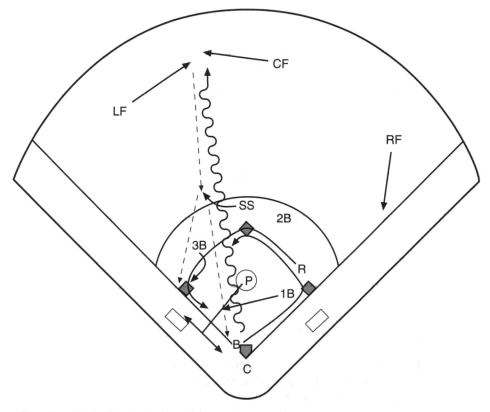

Situation 7—ball to left-center field.

2. *Ball to right-center field.* The third baseman goes to third base; the second baseman lines up the play for a possible relay at home. The short-stop trails the second baseman as a safety valve and calls the play by yelling "Home," "Third base," or "No play." The first baseman moves to the cutoff position around the mound. Initially, the pitcher backs up home plate. But if there is no play at home, he moves into position to back up third base. The left fielder is alert to back up third base.

3. *Ball to left-field corner.* The third baseman goes to third base and calls the play for the shortstop. He yells "4" for a throw to home, "3" for a throw to third base, "2" for a throw to second base, or simply "No play."

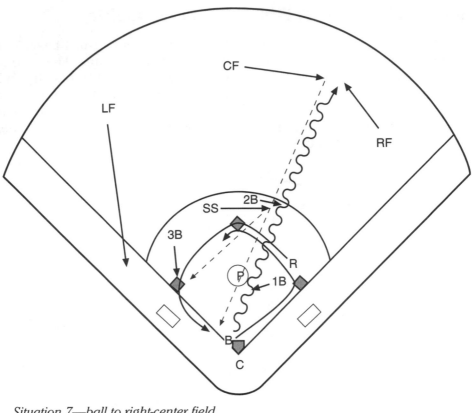

Situation 7—ball to right-center field.

The second baseman goes to second base, and the first baseman goes to the cutoff position along the third-base line. The pitcher backs up home plate in line with the throw to the plate. The right fielder is alert to cover second base.

4. *Ball to right-field corner.* The third baseman goes to third base; the second baseman and first baseman move to right-field line. The best arm takes the relay position for the play at the plate; the other is the safety valve and play caller. The shortstop goes to second base and, as the sure double develops, moves into cutoff position for a possible play at third base. The pitcher backs up third base. The left fielder is alert to back up third base. On a throw to the plate when the runner is safe, the catcher should go out and meet the ball for a possible play at third base.

Defense is the key to a competively great baseball team. The team that makes the fewest errors or mistakes will usually win the game. Normally the reasons for failure are improper positioning, inadequate anticipation of the circumstance, hurrying throws, and throwing off balance. The defensive performance chart provided on page 196 can help record the plays by each individual. To obtain competitive self-actualization a baseball team must emphasize defensive excellence.

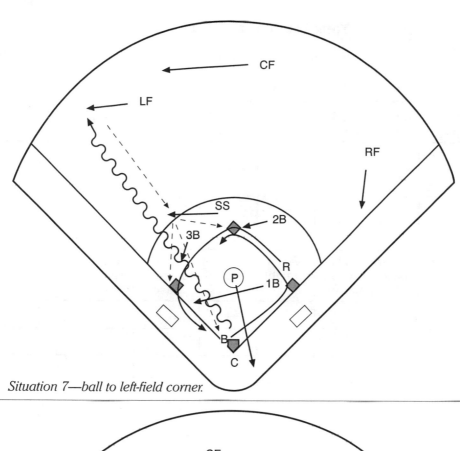

Situation 7—ball to left-field corner.

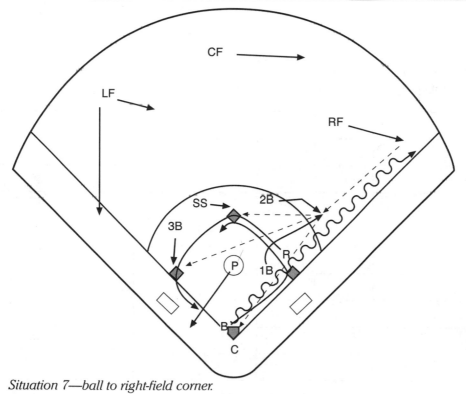

Situation 7—ball to right-field corner.

Your Team Name Here

Defensive Performance Chart

Key: + = succeeds, — = fails

Catcher	Back-up play	Block pitch	Block plate	Pop-up	Passed ball	Call play	Pick-off	PO-A-E	Total +/-

Pitcher	Back-up play	Cover base	Walk lead off batter	Walk 4 straight	Walk w/2outs	Throw to wrong base	Keep run close	PO-A-E	Total +/-

Infielders	Base coverage	Cut offs & relays	Commu-nications	Knock ball down	Hold runner	Throw to wrong base	Pick-offs	PO-A-E	Total +/-

Out-fielders	Back-up play	Cut offs & relays	Commu-nication	Charge ball	Drifts w/fly ball	Throw to wrong base	Too much time to throw	PO-A-E	Total +/-

12

Hitting

Baseball is the only field of endeavor where a man can succeed 3 times out of 10 and be considered a good performer.

H itting a baseball is considered one of the most difficult feats in sport. What makes it difficult is the danger involved every time the player goes to bat. Hitting requires good visualization, intense concentration, strength, quick bat speed, proper mechanics, patience, intelligence, and much practice. The hitter must squarely hit a round baseball traveling at 90 miles per hour on the sweet part of a round bat. Hitting a baseball is part physics and part instinct.

We believe that the outcome of a time at bat is determined before the event. In the one-on-one battle between pitcher and hitter, if either player gives in mentally, the result is to concede the outcome. Mental toughness and concentration are crucial to successful hitting.

In 1993 Tim Salmon, the American League Rookie of the Year, said, "I can't control the pitcher, the ball, the fielders, or the crowd, so I must be in control of myself. My routine not only prepares me physically but mentally creates the same frame of mind every time."

Great hitters learn to overcome adversity because they know they fail more than they succeed. All successful hitters are willing to risk failure, yet they hate to fail. They are persistent and determined, yet willing to acknowledge temporary defeat and prepare positively when at bat. The measure of a hitter's potential depends on how he handles adversity. Hitters must be mentally tough! They must have no fear of failure yet hate it passionately.

College coaches and pro scouts carefully watch players after they strike out or make an error. They want to see how the player handles it. Does he overcome adversity, or does he lose control when he makes a mistake or has a poor at bat? The answer often determines the player's potential for college recruitment and the professional draft. Professional scouts call this "makeup" because it answers the question, "What is he made of?"

Visual Component of Hitting

Of all elements of hitting, the visual component is often the most neglected, least taught, and most seldom practiced. Vision affects 80 percent of a ballplayer's performance. The three most important tools for the performance of baseball players are running speed, arm strength, and vision. Of these tools, vision is paramount.

When a hitter gets in a groove, the ball seems twice its normal size. Other times it comes to the plate looking like a golf ball. It doesn't matter how the batter feels either. He can feel great and not hit a thing, then feel lousy and hit it over the fence.

In the blink of an eye, quicker than it takes to read this sentence, in a nearly inconceivable .41 seconds, a major-league pitcher can throw the baseball past the batter. While the pitcher is winding up, the batter's brain must analyze game strategy and the pitcher's body language to determine speed and trajectory.

Hitting Objectives

Like any other task worthy of time and effort, hitting must have measurable objectives. We set these objectives for our hitters.

1. To hit the ball every time, that is, to strikeout less than 8 percent of the at bats
2. To hit line drives and hard ground balls at least 35 percent of the time
3. To hit the ball hard without trying to hit the baseball far
4. To be mentally ready to hit every pitch during every at bat

The analysis and decision phase, as the ball covers just over half the distance from the pitcher's mound to home plate, lasts just .21 seconds. The batter has just that tiny instant to respond. The batter's eyes track the ball as it leaves the pitcher's hand. Signals flash from the batter's retinas and along the optic nerves to the visual cortex at the back of the brain.

The visual cortex sends messages to the frontal association area of the cerebral cortex where information is analyzed. The brain's cerebral cortex integrates information, determines speed and trajectory, and activates impulses across the motor cortex that controls movement of the limbs. By some calculations, good hitters need .27 seconds to see, analyze, decide, and direct and .20 seconds to swing the bat (see diagram below).

Release to contact time at 90 miles per hour is .41 seconds, whereas the average swing time is .28 seconds and the fastest swing time is .17 seconds. When the .27 seconds needed for anticipation and perception is considered, it is obvious that he batter must make major adjustments.

With pitch-release to contact time at .45 seconds (78 to 80 miles per hour) to .41 seconds (90 miles per hour) and the average bat-swing time of .28 seconds (the fastest bat swing is .18 seconds), the time available to decide whether to swing or take is between .17 seconds and .21 seconds.

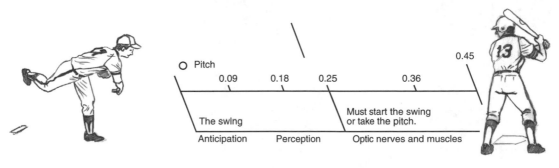

Response time.

Because all decisions are made in the first 30 to 45 feet, the batter must learn to pick up the baseball early for a longer look. Good hitters see the pitch and identify it between 6 and 8 feet out of the pitcher's hand. If it takes longer, the batter will fail.

The objective of the hitter is to find the ball earlier and see it longer, then create a mental image of the pitch trajectory that allows him to make contact without seeing the baseball hit the bat or cross the plate into the catcher's glove.

Carnegie Mellon University studies reveal that baseball players are more adept than ordinary people are at anticipating the paths of moving objects. This tracking skill separates baseball players from other athletes. At the 1985 United States Sport Festival in Baton Rogue, Louisiana, the ability to track moving objects blindly was tested, and baseball players excelled compared with other elite athletes.

Picking Up the Ball

The batter should visualize the pitch coming and see himself being successful. He can use the concept that the nervous system cannot tell the difference between what is real and what is imagined.

The hitter should study the pitcher for his release point from the on-deck circle or bench. If the pitcher uses an overhead windup, the release point will be about three-quarters higher. If the pitcher uses a chest-high windup, the release point will be lower, more of a sidearm delivery.

You can't hit if you don't swing.

At the plate the batter should ignore the pitcher's windup motion. He should use the eyes in a general manner by using a soft-center focus on one point, such as a number or a buckle, but not the pitcher's face. His attention should not be on anything specific until the moment of release. If the eye shift occurs too early, his vision will drift to center field and he won't see the ball well.

After the pitcher rocks and breaks his hands, the batter quickly shifts the eyes to the release point to clear the mind and fine-focus on the center of the ball. He must concentrate! He will see the ball better when he is aware of what he is seeing. In addition, he will lose tension and feel relaxed. The hitter should track the one-inch center of the ball as long as possible. To keep his eyes on the ball, he must not relax too soon.

The old adage that good hitters watch the ball all the way to the catcher's glove cannot possibly be true. The ball simply travels too fast. To do that, the hitter would have to jerk his eyes off the ball early in flight and then refocus on the ball as it speeds by him. The hitter should look for detail on the ball—spin, direction, and change in velocity. This ability can be learned! Depth perception is coachable as well.

If the hitter is successful in getting a base hit or taking a ball, he can relax and play it back to get a mental picture of his successful experience. If he fails, such swinging and missing, taking a good pitch, or swinging at a bad pitch, then he should replay the entire scene but change the result to a successful performance. The idea is to program the mind and body for success.

Good athletes communicate fundamentals and mechanics to the body with visual mental pictures. In reality, people see themselves doing things. Thus a visual image is more important than words.

Having a Plan at the Plate

The hitter must never waste a time at bat. They are precious. A major problem for young hitters is a lack of practice. Practice makes permanent. Batting is a constant battle of adjustments requiring tremendous experience. Every at bat, every time in the batter's box, warrants a game plan. The player should look forward enthusiastically to batting and getting a good pitch to hit. To accomplish this, he must learn the strike zone and then wait patiently for a good ball to hit. He must not become anxious and expand the strike zone for the pitcher. Patience is important. General U.S. Grant may have said it best: "The art of hitting is the art of getting a good ball to hit." The hitter should be sure that he has plate coverage so that he can hit any ball in his strike zone. Tony Gwynn, several times the National League batting champion, once said, "I wait and wait and let the ball get right on top of me and just swing with a loose grip." Proper thinking is 50 percent of effective hitting. The player should never be caught with the bat on his shoulder.

Being Aggressive

Aggressiveness is important. The batter must try to hurt the baseball when he hits it. His attitude must be fearless and self-confident. At the same time, he must maintain intensity and concentration so that he doesn't waste a time at bat. The most important results of hitting are to advance runners and drive in runs—that's what it's all about. Look for RBI hitters.

The hitter should say to himself, "Every pitch thrown is going to be a strike. I am going to hit every pitch." He should be ready to hit and not be surprised by a good pitch early in the count. Consider success in the count situation:

Zero strikes	.380 batting average
One strike	.324 batting average
Two strikes	.280 batting average

The hitter can anticipate the pitch by guessing logically, that is, by looking for the likely pitch.

0-0	68 percent fastballs
1-0	84 percent fastballs
2-0	93 percent fastballs
3-0	98 to 100 percent fastballs

You want hitters to make the logical guess, but you also know that some players do not have the concentration to study a pitcher enough to anticipate correctly. So, if a player is going to be a guess hitter, he should guess for a pitch he can mash!

I suggest that the studious hitter follow the example of Colorado Rockies superstar Todd Helton. He keeps a journal in which he charts every pitch in every at bat. This is part of his mental preparation to hit.

Being in Control

To succeed in baseball, a player must have total control of his emotions and absolute concentration. He should block out all negative thoughts and the things beyond his control while concentrating on the things he can control.

The effective hitter controls himself and gets on with the next pitch. Even great players are vulnerable if they don't focus on the next pitch or next at bat. If the hitter is still thinking about an umpire's bad call, he can't concentrate on the next pitch, the next at bat, or his play in the field. Errors often occur when players take their at bats with them to the field.

With two strikes the batter must make contact; therefore, he should choke up on the bat two inches for better control.

Watching the Signs

Players can learn to read the pitcher's action. Many tip their pitches. Batters should study the pitcher from both the dugout and the on-deck circle. They should look for different finger grips, especially from the set position, and variations in the windup and set position, especially for a higher set for the curveball and a lower set for the fastball.

Players can also learn to call pitches from second base and the dugout by watching the catcher's sign and his positioning behind the plate. They can then communicate either orally or with signs to their teammates.

Proper Preparation

Success or failure is largely determined before the at bat. We expect each player to develop a routine to prepare for every at bat. He uses this time to transform himself mentally and physically from a team member into a well-oiled hitting machine. Any act, such as putting on batting gloves or putting on a helmet, can trigger this metamorphosis. The player should initiate this process at least five batters before his at bat.

All choices in hitting involve both bat speed and accuracy. Of the two, the accuracy of the swing is more important. Decisions about hitting mechanics must consider the generation of maximum bat speed.

The contact point on the bat is the most important factor in hitting. This point is on the sweet part of the bat, that is, the center of percussion, or the node. To get better bat control, we recommend choking up about two inches. Choking up also promotes a quicker and more accurate swing. Many people fail to comprehend the significance of the contact point. Consider the hitter who bails out on an inside pitch but gets a base hit when the pitch hits the bat and the ball falls over the infielders.

In the On-Deck Circle

Most American baseball players swing with two or three bats or a weighted bat in the on-deck circle. I disapprove of this practice. Although the hitter may benefit from the feeling of lightness when he moves to a single bat, the earlier swinging of inordinate weight may alter coordination and bat control.

I recommend using one bat and concentrating on timing the pitcher and looking for his release point. The time in the on-deck circle should be used to prepare mentally. This is the closest the hitter will come to the pitcher before an at bat. Hall of Fame slugger Hank Aaron said, "I always focused on what the pitcher was doing when I was in the on-deck circle."

If a play occurs at the plate, the on-deck hitter becomes the home-plate coach. His duties include clearing the area so that the runner can slide safely and coaching the runner to slide.

Bat Selection

The hitter should select a bat that he can swing quickly and accurately. Of course, he should do this before the game. With the arm fully extended, the player holds the bat parallel to the ground with one hand. If the bat shakes, it is too heavy. He should try a bat without knowing its weight. In general, the lighter the bat, the better.

We recommend that bat selection be based on age, height, and weight (see table 12.1)

Try 32-inch bats for players five feet, five inches tall to five feet, eight inches tall and weighing between 100 and 120 pounds. The 33-inch bat is for players from five feet, five inches tall to six feet tall with a body weight of 120 to 170 pounds. And the 34-inch bat is for players five feet, nine inches tall to over six feet, one inch tall with a body weight of 160 to over 200 pounds.

Table 12.1 Bat Selection	
Age	Bat size (in inches)
11–12	30–31
13–14	31–32
15–16	32–33

Hitting the Ball

A lot of factors go into getting a base hit and it all starts with how you hold the bat, your stance and position at the plate, and the way you swing at the pitch.

Grip

The hands should be strong and quick, but the grip should be soft and relaxed with the bat held in the fingers, not the palms. Proper knuckle alignment must allow for freedom of movement. This is best accomplished with the golfer's grip. The door-knocking knuckles are aligned. This grip allows the development of maximum bat speed. To feel this, the player should swing the bat like a whip, using various knuckle alignments. Done correctly, the action will be smooth and fast.

Location in the Batter's Box

The hitter first steps in with the back foot parallel to the pitcher's rubber and deep in the box, with the foot on the line. The front foot is also paral-

Hitting grip.

Location in the batter's box.

lel. The distance of the stance from home plate should be equal to the length of the bat when measured from the middle of home plate.

The location should be such that at contact the front foot is even with the front edge of home plate. This position allows the umpire to establish a true strike zone.

Mechanics

There are several key points to having good mechanics. Consider the following guidelines.

1. Balance is the most important fundamental of good batting mechanics. Balance is defined as the rotation of the batter's center of gravity relative to his base. Using a parallel stance with the feet spread wide apart, the hitter keeps the weight forward on the balls of the feet toward the toes, which are straight ahead. The posture should be relaxed and erect with a vertical torso. Ankles are flexed and knees are deeply flexed. The hitter positions himself as he would when sitting in a chair, covering the feet with a wide stance spread twice the width of the shoulders. He turns to look at the pitcher with his eyes level and his head up. The waist should bend slightly toward the plate, with the front shoulder slightly lower than the back shoulder.

2. With the door-knocking knuckles aligned, the hands are near the rear of the chest, not more than four to six inches from the body. Hands held farther away produce a sweeping swing. The correct hand position is in the top of the strike zone, comfortable, strong, and back. Both elbows are down to force a short, quick stroke. The bat will follow in the plane of the front elbow, so the hitter must keep the elbow down. The back elbow is relaxed and lower than the shoulder. An elevated back elbow creates tension and inhibits bat speed.

3. The hitter gets the bat started by using rhythm and movement in the

Hand position.

Launching position.

stance. The key is to control the start of the swing with the lower body, not the hands. He must be careful not to wrap the bat. If he does, he will become a bottom-hand hitter. As a timing mechanism, hitching is OK if as the pitcher's hands start down, the hitter's hands start down, and as the pitcher's hands start up, the hitter's hands start up.

4. The bat should be held at a 45-degree angle over the back shoulder, thereby putting the bat in launching position when the front foot touches down. The bottom hand must be in the radial deviation position with the wrist fully extended and back near the rear shoulder. On the trigger, or takeaway, the batter gets a controlled inward total-body turn of the shoulder, hip, and knee so that the hands start moving. When the pitcher shows his hip pocket, the batter shows him his hip pocket. Again, the batter must not wrap the bat or lose vision from the rear eye.

5. The weight shift, especially the explosive hip rotation, initiates the swing. The weight shift begins from a firm, rigid backside and moves forward to a firm, rigid front side. The shift occurs at 50 percent of stride length. This torque is generated by the flexion to extension of the abdominal oblique muscles, legs, and buttocks. Hitters need to understand that the rotational force of the body generates bat speed. The navel should face the ball, not the pitcher, when the hitter finishes. The back leg must not break down (collapse). The hitter must maintain bal-

Note how the hips shift here.

ance when transferring his weight, going only as far as to keep the head four to six inches behind the closed front foot.

6. The hitter take either no stride or a short stride of less than four inches with a closed front foot. The simple short-stride technique allows the hitter more time to wait on the ball, whereas a long stride forces him to start the swing earlier. If the hitter uses the no-stride style, the weight should already be on the inside of the feet. If the shift occurs too soon, the front arm extends too early, producing a sweeping swing. This long, slow swing often results in strikeouts. If the hitter steps, he simply picks up his foot and puts it back down quickly, landing on the inside of the front foot to keep his weight back.

7. The swing path is a positive, assertive motion directed toward the pitcher. The hands should move like a pendulum and remain inside the ball during the swing. The initial hand movement should be toward the sternum. "Hands to the heart" or "Butt of the bat to the ball" are coaching points. The bottom hand must seem as if it is stabbing someone's butt with the end of the bat. By keeping the wrist flexed and the side of the bottom hand toward the ball, the front elbow stays down, thereby promoting a compact swing inside the ball.

Swing path.

Form a flexed V with arms.

8. To complete the swing, the player uses a relaxed, compact motion with full arm extension toward the pitcher. (A flexed V should be formed with the arms, shoulder, to a wrist). The hitter must start the bat sooner on an inside pitch because that is the only way to get the sweet part of the bat on the ball. At the point of contact the hands should be in the palm-up, palm-down position. The difference in hitting an inside pitch versus an outside pitch is that the hitter must start sooner on the inside pitch. He should use a quick, powerful wrist action. The power source for bat-head speed comes from flexion to extension.

9. The hitter keeps the chin and eyes down when swinging. He focuses on the ball, attempting to watch it all the way to the bat even though doing so is physiologically impossible. He should create a mental picture. He keeps the head still and uses a tracking action of the eyes to force his head and eyes to follow the ball into the catcher's glove. He must concentrate on every swing.

10. The player should learn to use the entire field by hitting the ball where it is pitched and aiming for the hitting lanes. The theory of Baltimore Orioles Hall of Fame outfielder Wee Willie Keeler applies here: "Hit it where they ain't." The hitter should be able to adjust to all types and speeds of pitches by maintaining balance.

11. By releasing the top hand, the hitter will find it easier to hit through the ball to maximum extension toward the pitcher without rolling the wrist on contact. As he follows through to extension, he remains

Follow-through.

balanced to the concluding position. The hands are above the shoulder, and the eyes are down. A very high and late release of the top hand will help promote a relaxed, rhythmical swing.

Common Faults of Young Hitters

1. Failing to keep the head down at contact, referred to as "opening up too soon," will cause the head and front side to fly out and away from the ball.
2. Extending the hands out and away from the body will cause the bat to be swung around the ball. The hitter will hit the outside part of the ball and will often show great foul-ball power to the pull side of the field.

Bunting

Bunting is an essential part of the hitter's repertoire, whether sacrificing or bunting for a hit. You should insist that all players on your club learn to drag, push, sacrifice, and slash bunt. When your players have these skills, you have a total package. Bunting can upset the defense, help the team, improve a batting average, and prevent a slump. Work on bunting daily in practice and encourage your players to bunt in games. Bunting is one of the skills of the complete player.

Pivot-style bunting technique.

Sacrifice Bunting

The desire to bunt is the most important factor in determining bunting success. Players must know the bunt sign and accept it without emotion. They should have the attitude of going to the plate intent on making an out to help their team. Coaches must not overuse the sacrifice bunt so that players learn that sacrificing is important to team play.

The bunt is made from the front part of the batter's box. The batter moves closer to the pitcher to improve the angles, as far as 18 inches into fair territory. The batter should not show the bunt play too early, before the pitcher sets. He looks for a pitch in the upper half of the strike zone and must keep both eyes on the pitched ball.

When bunting, the batter bends the knees slightly, keeping the elbows down and close to the body with the bat at a 45-degree angle as he concentrates on the strike zone. The barrel end of the bat is higher than the handle end. The grip on the bat is loose, with the fingers behind the barrel.

The batter bunts the top half of the ball out in front of the body. The bat action is backward. "Give with the pitch!" is a useful coaching cue. The batter should allow the bat to absorb the force of the pitch and deaden it. The action is similar to catching the ball, but with a bat, not a glove.

The direction of the bunt is an important aspect of a successful sacrifice. On a sacrifice bunt the batter must concentrate and keep the ball away from the pitcher. With a runner on first base, the bunt should be down the first-base line. With a runner on second base, the bunt should be down the third-base line. The batter must not break too quickly away from the plate; he must be certain that he has bunted the ball. First things first: Bunt before you run. The batter should bunt strikes and take balls. A base on balls will advance runners as well as a sacrifice does.

Slash Bunt

With runners on first and second, the slash bunt, also known as the butcher-boy play, is a good play, but it requires a great deal of skill. To execute the slash bunt, the hitter slides the hands up the bat about six inches and shows the bunt, then takes away with a coil action and swings. For maximum effectiveness, the slash bunt should be used only in obvious bunt situations, when it will cause the infielders to move out of position and create confusion.

Bunting for a Hit

The drag bunt is used in five situations: when the hitter is slumping, when the defense concedes the hit, when you want to alter the depth of the third baseman, in place of a sacrifice bunt, and with a special offensive play.

The drag bunt should never be used with runners on base unless they are aware it is on. Always have a sign for the drag bunt. To execute the drag bunt, the batter shortens up on the bat with both hands while keeping the barrel high with the top hand higher than the bottom. Right-handed bunters should adjust forward in the batter's box so that they can drop step, then jab step with the front foot. Left-handed batters also move up in the box and closer to the plate. Lefties look for an inside pitch. The bunter should not step with the front foot. He bunts the ball and then uses the crossover step to run.

When bunting for a hit, the bunt should be down the third-base line. That way, if the ball rolls foul it is only a strike. Also, the bunter should try to keep the ball away from the pitcher. The result should be a hit or a foul ball, never an out.

The bunter should study the pitcher's follow-through so that he can bunt for a hit using either the drag bunt or the push bunt. The idea is to bunt away from the pitcher. The golden rule is to make a perfect bunt or foul it off. A perfect right-handed drag bunt and a perfect left-handed push bunt will go inside the foul line but no more than three feet fair.

When attempting a drag or push bunt, the bunter must get the ball past the pitcher in an approximate line toward the second baseman. The bunter must not run too soon; he must bunt the ball before he can run. A right-hander's drag-bunting technique must be executed to place the ball down the third-base line. As the pitcher delivers the pitch, the bunter points the bat at the first baseman. At the same time, he should take a drop step back with the right foot.

The right-handed push bunt is used when the first baseman plays too deep. The bunter should take a short jab step with his left foot and push the outside pitch hard enough to get it past the pitcher toward first.

The left-handed drag bunt is used when the first baseman plays too deep. The initial step is toward the third baseman with the right foot. The bat head is pointed at the third baseman. The ball is bunted with the intention to bunt the ball past the pitcher, forcing the second baseman or first baseman to field it. On the left-handed push bunt down the third-base line, the first step is made with the front foot. The ball is then bunted softly.

Suicide Squeeze

Timing is crucial in executing the suicide squeeze. The batter must be careful not to show the bunt too early, and the runner must not start too early. The proper time for the batter to square and for the runner at third to break is when the pitcher's front foot touches down.

The batter should place the bunt to the pitcher's glove side. Because he is giving himself up, he must bunt the ball into fair territory and on the ground.

Shadow Squeeze

The batter shows the bunt early and bunts the ball to the third baseman. As the third baseman moves in to field the bunt, the runner on third shadows him. If the third baseman throws to first, the runner scores. If the third baseman holds the ball, the runner retreats to third base and the batter reaches safely.

Fake Bunt and Steal

The batter must set up deep in the batter's box for the fake bunt and steal. He should square to show bunt when the pitcher breaks his hands. The batter should try to place the barrel of the bat in the catcher's line of vision. As the pitch arrives, the batter reaches out and then moves the bat backward toward the catcher, keeping the bat in the catcher's line of vision as long as possible. At the last instant, he pulls the bat upward and out of the strike zone.

Safety Squeeze

The best time to use the safety squeeze is with runners at first and third bases with no outs. The batter executes a bunt for a hit, and then the runners react to the defensive option.

Hitting Drills

One of the secrets of hitting is waiting. The key to waiting is to have strong hands. We recommend using the overload-underload principle. Specifically, we suggest that our players swing both a weighted bat and a fungo bat 100 times a day with each hand. That is 400 swings daily, or more than 2,000 swings each week. Players should work on the quick, compact stroke, using the mechanics of positive procedures. This method will develop the muscular fitness needed to be an excellent hitter.

When learning a new skill or technique, players should perform it slowly and repetitively. To learn to compete, we practice hitting against quality pitching. As often as practical, players should face live pitching from the mound with a catcher. The pitcher should throw hard strikes using all pitches while telling the hitter what is coming. This method should be done at full speed, using modified gamelike conditions. The following drills are progressive, intended to improve performance.

Freeze Checkpoints

Purpose: To teach the proper mechanics of hitting

Implementation:

1. The batter takes a dry swing at an imaginary pitch. Then, when completing the follow-through, he freezes so that he can complete the checklist.
2. He self-evaluates the following points:

- Closed front foot
- Back foot pivoted
- Complete rear-shoulder follow-through
- Head down looking at the point of contact
- A-frame with the lower body so that the head is over the back knee
- Finish of the swing high with the bottom hand

Batting-Tee Drill

Purpose: To learn the mechanics of hitting

Implementation:
1. Set up a batting tee at home plate. Elevate the ball to the top of the strike zone. Put a hula hoop on the pitcher's mound or hang it in the batting cage at 60 feet, 6 inches to simulate normal depth perception.
2. First, the batter visualizes the pitcher on the mound 60 feet, 6 inches away. Then he imagines the ball coming toward him. He hits the middle of the ball with the best possible mechanics.
3. The Tony Gwynn variation is to hit the baseball to the opposite field between the third baseman and the shortstop, the 5.5 hole.

Dry Swings With Pauses

Purpose: To learn the mechanics of hitting

Implementation:
1. The batter assumes the best possible batting stance. He checks to see that the back foot is parallel to the pitching rubber, that the knee and ankle have proper flexion, and that his upper body is relaxed.
2. He moves to the power position. He checks to see that the bottom hand is flexed and that the bat is at about 45 degrees, with the barrel of the bat near the back of the helmet (not wrapped).
3. He swings by keeping the hands inside the ball, then stops at the point of contact. He checks that the hands are palm up and palm down and that the head is down and over the rear knee.
4. He finishes the swing to a proper follow-through. He checks for a closed front foot, a back-foot pivot, a completed rear-shoulder action, a low head, a balanced center of gravity with the head over the rear knee, and a one-handed high finish.

Tracking Slowly-Pitched Tennis Balls

Purpose: To develop hand-eye coordination

Implementation:
1. This drill requires a dozen tennis balls with numbers printed on two sides of each ball large enough to be easily seen. Have a player pitch the tennis balls to a hitter from a distance of 60 feet at slow to moderate speed.
2. The hitter takes a good batting stance, holding the bat with only his bottom hand. The hitter attempts to track the ball with his eyes so that he can read the number on the ball. When he reads the number, he calls it out.
3. At the same time, he should hit the ball using the one-handed swing.

Soft Toss or Screen Ball

Purpose: To learn the fundamentals of hitting

Implementation:
1. The hitter assumes his stance about 10 feet from the net. A partner is slightly in front and off to the side of the hitter.
2. This drill must be well coordinated for maximum success. As the partner begins to toss the baseball, the hitter moves to the launch position. The partner tosses the baseball on a flat plane into the strike zone.
3. The hitter attempts to use perfect technique to hit a line drive into the net.
4. The partners repeat the tosses and swings for 10 pitches, then exchange places.

Variations:
- To teach hitting a curveball, the partner tosses the ball high so that it drops into the strike zone.
- The partner fakes a toss to teach the hitter to stay balanced and back, that is, not to lunge.
- The partner moves to the rear and does rear tosses to teach the steps of the swing in two parts, that is, the load and the swing to follow-through. If the batter were at home plate the tosser would be in the catcher's box. The hitter looks back and loads. The tosser tosses the ball toward the pitcher's mound while the batter swings will full extension toward the hitter.

Live Batting Practice

Purpose: To teach the hitter to compete

Implementation:

1. Everything is done at full speed to make this drill gamelike. Never use this drill to work on the mechanics of hitting!
2. Always use a catcher in full equipment and pitch from the mound at the full distance of 60 feet, 6 inches.
3. Before the pitch the pitcher communicates to the hitter the type of pitch he is throwing—fastball, curveball, slider, and so on. Then he throws the pitch for a strike so that the hitter can hit it. He must not try to fool the hitter or strike him out.
4. The hitter attempts to use the previous learning to take a fundamentally sound swing and hit the baseball in the middle.
5. Allow each batter to take only five swings or see only eight pitches per turn at bat.

Variations:

- The hitter looks for pitches to hit a ground ball to the right side of the field.
- The hitter looks for pitches up in the strike zone to hit fly balls.
- The batter hits the ball after it passes home plate, directing it at a right angle into the dugout with the goal of learning to wait as long as possible. This is sometimes called backside, two-strike hitting.
- Target practice. The hitter tries to hit the three bases.
- To execute the contact play, the batter hits ground balls six feet in front of the plate

Methods of Assessment

- *Method 1.* We use a point system in practice as a quality-control technique (see table 12.2).
- *Method 2.* Use slugging average for evaluation rather than batting average. Slugging average is determined by dividing total bases by the number of at bats.
- *Method 3.* Self-evaluation. The player can evaluate himself with four checkpoints at the point of contact, which is even with the front foot.

    1. The rear foot "squashes the roach."
    2. The front foot remains closed.

Table 12.2	Point System	
Points	**Types of hit**	**Projected batting average**
8	Line drive	.788
6	Hard ground ball	.568
2	Swinging bunt	.226
2	Long fly ball	.196
2	Routine ground ball	.170
1	Routine fly ball	.071
0	Strike out	.000

3. The rear shoulder and the chin are close when the head is down.
4. The front shoulder is closed.

Baseball in the only field of endeavor where a man can succeed three times out of ten and is considered a good performer. By hitting consistently, the base hits will take care of themselves.

13

Baserunning

*The best player on the team is usually
the best base runner.*

Without exception, explosiveness is important in baseball. Whether a player is diving for a ball or accelerating from first base in an attempt to steal second, success depends on explosive ability. Professional scouts refer to this as a quick first step, or two-step quickness.

The best indicator of general athletic ability is running speed. By improving speed, the player can improve all-around baseball ability. Speed is an essential element to offensive success, baserunning, and defensive performance. Improved speed can mean a higher batting average. The difference between a .250 hitter and a .300 hitter is just 1 hit in every 20 at bats. Improved speed can mean more stolen bases. Quickness of foot and mind are the chief factors in baserunning. Improved speed can mean better defensive range. Speed and quickness are prerequisites to making the big play! Improved speed can create an aggressive offense that will cause the defense to hurry throws and make mistakes. Speed can put pressure on the opponent, and some of them will break under the pressure.

Organization

Many baseball people know that the best baseball player on the team is usually the best base runner. This is an important fact. If the player wants to show off his skill, he must dominate with speed.

Team selection based on speed is a philosophical commitment. A long time ago, I learned that those with speed usually win. Therefore, seek speedy athletes for your team. The first test administered in major-league baseball tryout camps, as in my own, is the 60-yard dash.

Coaching Points

1. Teaching of proper sprinting techniques should be included in every practice.
2. Clock all hitters to first base and base stealers to second. The stopwatch won't lie. The numbers are objective.
3. Ninety percent of base running is on the player's initiative rather than being dependent on base coaches. Good base running is common sense, but the player must think about it ahead of time. The base runner should consider all possible situations and execute whatever is in order.

A Trip Around the Bases

Good baserunning begins with careful study in the dugout and progresses around the bases with fundamentals, skills, strategies, and techniques specific to a given situation. This next section offers tips on the little things necessary to know what to do and when to do it.

In the Dugout

The player in the dugout has much to do. He can study the pitcher's motion to home plate, the pitcher's set position, the pickoff plays. He should evaluate the strength of the outfielders' arms and know which arm each throws with. He can determine the shortstop's and second baseman's usual pivots on double plays. By studying the positioning of infielders and outfielders, he may find a mistake to exploit. For example, if the outfielder catches the ball on his glove side, the runner should consider taking an extra base. The hitter in the hole should get his helmet and bat immediately so he is ready to go to the on-deck circle.

On Deck

The player on deck has the job of helping the base runner score at home plate. If there is time, he cleans the home-plate area of equipment, such as the bat or catcher's mask. He should be in easy sight of the runner but position himself far enough away to avoid interference. Remember, once the slide sign has been given, the runner cannot change his mind.

At Home Plate

Reiterate the importance of proper mental preparation for hitting with your players. Before stepping into the batter's box, the hitter must look at the coach to take the signs. Immediately after every pitch the hitter must step out with one foot and look for the coach's signs. At the same time, runners should immediately return to their bases and look for signs.

If the batter intends to bunt, he must remember that the key to bunting is desire. He can move while the pitcher is in his windup, but after that he should be still. He can use a check swing to disrupt the catcher.

Running at Any Base

Whether the player is the batter-runner or a runner at any base, he must always watch the runner or runners in front of him and know their speed and base-running ability. It is better to stay at a base rather than be caught in a rundown.

During a rundown a runner should always try to advance a base if there are less than two outs. If there are two outs, a baserunner should try to give the trapped runner two bases so that he has an opportunity to escape.

Runners must learn to read pitched balls in the dirt off the secondary lead. When the pitcher throws home, the runner takes the secondary

Look for opportunities to advance a base on a wild pitch.

lead by using two shuffle steps. If the runner reads that the trajectory of the batted ball is down, he takes one more slide and reacts. He may be able to advance a base because of a wild pitch.

Rounding Bases

The runner must always touch each base. If he misses one, he should go back and touch it. Touching the base with either foot is acceptable. Some contend

When rounding a base, turn the head sharply in the direction of the next base.

A good lead versus a right-handed pitcher.

that touching the bases with the left foot and banking against it is the better method, but we believe that the runner should not break stride to accommodate touching the base.

We have discovered that the key to rounding a base is turning the head toward the next base. Where the head goes, the body follows. If the player turns his head sharply as he touches the base, he tends to run in a less elliptical path. If the runner looks toward the outfield, the path will be wider as the runner drifts toward a more circular path.

Running at First Base

The key to getting extra-base hits is for the batter-runner to avoid stopping himself rather than being concerned about the defense stopping him. The first two steps out of the box will determine the chance for extra bases. The batter-runner must know which arm each outfielder throw with so that he can advance an extra base when the ball is on the glove side.

Batter-Runner to First Base

After the batter hits the ball, by rule he is called the batter-runner. Here are some guidelines to follow on the way to first base.

The player should run in a straight line to the base; however, the batter-runner must run the last 45 feet in the box so that he is not called out for interference. Interference can be either physical contact with the thrown ball or mere visual interference that blocks a fielder's view at first base. The runner should occasionally slide into first base to avoid being tagged out by the first baseman. By watching the first baseman's feet, the runner can determine if a slide would be helpful. If the first baseman comes down the line, the slide should be in foul territory.

The player should always run through first base on ground balls. As he touches first base, he leans forward, then looks over his shoulder for the ball. The first-base coach has no need to tell runners to run because the runner can easily see the play. If the runner sees the ball go past the first baseman, he must break down by spreading out the feet to slow down.

When making the turn around the bag, the runner must be aggressive and not break his stride. He should make a big turn. If the outfielder throws behind him, he should advance to the next base.

On fly balls the runner should anticipate an error. He should end up on second whether or not the fielder catches the ball. Running hard on fly balls is a measure of attitude and desire to compete. On hits to the outfield, the runner should carefully watch the ball and make sure that the cutoff throw goes past the cutoff man before he advances. In general, if the outfielder's throw is low, the runner stays and spies. If the throw is high in the air, he takes the extra base.

At First Base

Once the runner reaches first base and stops, he must quickly assess the game and watch for a variety of elements. First and foremost, know where the ball is! You can't be tagged out without the ball. Know the overall situation at hand—how many outs in the inning, where the defense is playing in the field—and be ready to play with instinct. Check the coach's signs while on base then take a lead, but don't wait until the pitcher is on the rubber. Be alert for any hidden-ball tricks and avoid visiting with the first baseman and coach.

Leading Off First

Every situation calls for a different lead off. The runner should be alert and decide whether or not a steal is okay. It's always better to play it safe. The runner should lead off the outfield side (corner) of the base in a direct line to second, keeping in mind that all leads are a race between himself and the baseball. The player should remember that he can't steal second base by keeping his foot on first. There are three main types of first-move leads:

- **One-way lead.** The purpose of the one-way lead is to draw a throw to set up a steal. The runner takes a big lead with the weight on the left foot. He watches the ball. With any movement by the pitcher the runner takes a crossover step and then reacts to the ball. He should be prepared to dive by using a finger-first slide.

- **Two-way lead.** The five-step two-way lead is our fundamental measured technique. The runner takes the maximum lead with five measured steps, normally 12 to 14 feet. Slowly and deliberately, he moves directly toward second base using a jab step, crossover step, slide, slide, and slide steps. The hands are up at chest level, and the posture is erect. The feet are shoulder-width apart with the knees bent, and the eyes are on the pitcher. This is the so-called athletic position, which must be an explosive and powerful position.

- **Walking lead.** On walking leads, however, the runner keeps his eyes on the ball and reacts to what happens. He must be ready to slide! This timing technique combined with the reading of cues will enable him to get a great jump on the pitcher. The concept is simply to get a running start. The body in motion tends to stay in motion.

For leads against a left-handed pitcher, the runner takes a large five-step lead and watches the ball. On any movement by the pitcher, he takes a jab step with the left foot back toward first base and then reacts to the ball. We use this lead to set up a first-move steal.

For the secondary lead, the movement occurs as the pitcher starts to deliver the ball to the hitter. The runner uses two shuffle steps toward second base to extend the lead. At this point he must be ready to return quickly to first or react to the batted ball. This movement sets up the delayed steal.

When returning to the base, the runner moves back to the base on any movement by the pitcher toward the base. He pushes the left arm down and toward right field, uses the crossover step, and drives. Diving back is necessary. The player should have no fear of getting a dirty uniform. He touches the far corner of the base with the right hand. If the runner returns standing up, he puts his right elbow up to brace the first baseman and touches the far corner of the base with his right foot.

General Guidelines

Sometimes people call it "good baseball instincts," while others call it "alert hands up" play. If you follow these simple base-running guidelines, you will exhibit those respected skills. Remember, always force the defense by moving up. Look for wild pitches and passed balls. If the pitches are low, cheat to the next base. If a double-play is in order, be mentally prepared to break it up, however, it is important to know the league rules on this as it varies from league to league. With runners on first and third, runners tag up on all foul fly balls to create a defensive problem. When attempting to beat the force out at second base, the runner should take pride in his ability to get a good jump on a ground ball. He may beat the infielder to the base. The runner should also be conscious of the double steal with a runner at second. He runs from first when his teammate breaks for third. Because most defenses play for the lead runner, the runner at first will not need a good jump.

- **Fly balls to left field, center field, or left-center field.** The runner should go as far as possible to second base. He may even pass second base. He anticipates the error or hit and expects to score or at least get to third base if the ball is misplayed.

- **Sliding.** Runners should use the fingers-first slide on all tag plays except at home plate, where this is considered dangerous because catchers often block the plate. Runners must be especially prepared to slide on a steal attempt. However, the runner should use the pop-up slide when possible so that he can quickly advance.

- **Advancing to second base.** When advancing to second base with the ball behind him, such as in right field, the runner picks up the third-base coach for help. Still, he must remember that 90 percent of running is his responsibility. He should look, touch, look—look before he gets to second, touch second, and look again at the coach. He should remember to turn his head quickly toward third to reduce the distance that he will have to run to get there.

When making his turn around second base, he doesn't drift by the base because doing so makes him vulnerable to the outfielder throwing the ball behind him. We prefer that the runner stop on second base rather than make the turn.

- **Advancing on the bunt.** When advancing on the bunt, the runner should look at the baseball during his secondary lead. The ball must be on the ground before he runs. The running bunt play is designed for the runner to advance two bases on the sacrifice bunt. The runner steals on the pitch as the batter executes a bunt to the third baseman. If the third baseman moves in to field the bunt, the runner can advance to third. The fake bunt and steal is a special play that we reserve for crucial situations. On this play the bunter attempts to hide the ball from the catcher's view as long as possible. He then moves the bat back toward the catcher, trying to hide the ball behind the bat. Finally, he pulls the bat up and out of the strike zone. The ball should appear to explode onto the catcher and make throwing awkward.

Stealing Second Base

A successful steal of second base can be accomplished in several ways. These tips about stealing will be useful to your players. Accelerate from the start by using the crossover step toward second. Use the hand-first slide and touch the back corner of the base and remember to accelerate within the slide by sliding at full speed. Try to steal the catcher's sign so that you can steal on a slower pitch, such as a breaking ball. For example, the front elbow is a good cue. If the elbow tucks, the pitcher is throwing to the plate. If the elbow opens to first base, it is a pickoff. The front foot is another good cue. If the left foot lifts, it is a pitch. If the left foot opens to first base, it is a pickoff.

Cues to Stealing on a Right-Handed Pitcher

By studying the pitcher's delivery while you're on the bench, you can identify cues for throwing home versus throwing to first base. For example, if the pitcher is opened in the set position to first base, he must wheel to throw home; therefore, the baserunner can run when the left shoulder moves away. Once the pitcher starts away from first he cannot throw to first base. If he does, it is a balk. If the pitcher is a high kicker, the basestealer can run when the pitcher's left knee bends. However, if the pitcher does neither, the baserunner must steal on the pitcher's foot movement. When the left foot moves and the right heel moves up, or if

Left shoulder opened toward first base while in set position.

Left shoulder moved in—pitch is going home.

To home—left heel up, back heel down.   *To first base—front heel down, back heel up.*

both feet are close together, a pickoff play is coming. But if both feet move, the right heel stays down, and his body leans forward, the pitcher is going to the plate.

Cues to Stealing on a Left-Handed Pitcher

There are several cues to look for when watching a pitcher for the pitch versus for the pickoff.

• **The pitch.** When the pitcher curls the foot or front knee back, puts his chin down, and leans his body forward, he is delivering a pitch. If he is looking at first base as he starts his delivery, he's going to home plate. The runner can look for the pitcher's right foot breaking the back plane of the rubber. Once the foot breaks that plane, he must deliver a pitch. If he throws to first, it is a balk. Also keep in mind that a glove in a low set may indicate a pitch, whereas a high set would mean a pickoff.

• **The pickoff.** When the chin is up, the toe is pointed toward first base, the front knee is straight up, the body leans backward, and the stance between the legs is wide, the throw is coming to first. We call this reading the gap. When he is looking at the batter, he is coming to first for a pickoff. The baserunner should also look for for differences in speed of motion. A quick motion means a pitch, whereas a slow motion is a throw to first base. We call this tempo pitching.

Left-handed pitcher looking to first base—throwing home.

Left-handed pitcher looking home— throwing to first base.

The steal of second is attempted in the following three ways.

1. In the **direct steal,** a runner is given a sign to steal and he must attempt to steal. We seldom use this play in my ball club. Most frequently, it is used to force timid runners to steal.

2. The **delayed steal** is effective when the shortstop and second baseman are too far from the base to cover it easily, against infielders who have the habit of relaxing after a pitch, when the opponent doesn't expect the runner to steal, or when the catcher has the habit of dropping to his knees to return the ball to the pitcher. In the delayed steal, the runner executes an extended secondary lead. He takes three shuffles and gains as much distance as he can. When the pitch reaches the hitting zone, the runner breaks for second base. When teaching the delayed steal, we use the verbal teaching cues "Shuffle, shuffle, shuffle, run."

3. The **indirect steal** is a call for a possible steal. When our runners get the sign for the indirect steal, they know they can steal on any pitch if they feel they can get both a good lead and a good jump on the pitch. If they fail to get both, they don't run.

Once the runner commits and breaks to second, he uses the crossover step to start toward second. On the fourth step, we want the runner to peek at the pitch to see if the ball is batted or not. He can then react to anything that happens, such as a wild pitch or pop-up.

The most difficult aspect of the indirect steal is for the ballplayer to understand that he doesn't have to run. He has the option of running as long as the situation remains the same. He must be daring and willing to challenge people. In our ball club, we use this play often. In some cases, the indirect steal is automatic for certain runners.

A note of caution is that the runner is often unaware of where the pitched ball was thrown. If the ball is thrown in the dirt, some sly and devious infielders will tell the runner, "Foul ball, go back to first." Some instinctively challenged baserunners will return to first and become vulnerable to being put out.

Special Plays, Runners at First and Third

There are various types of exciting and creative plays with runners on first and third. A complete offensive package will include many plays. If successful, the play will result in one run scored and a runner on second base.

1. The **straight double steal** is the basic play in the first-and-third situation. The runner at first attempts a direct steal of second, while the runner on third breaks for the plate when the catcher's throw to second goes past the pitcher.

2. The **walking double steal** begins with any three-ball count on the hitter and a runner at third. If the pitch is called ball four, the batter is awarded first base. When the batter-runner touches first, he initiates the double steal play by sprinting to second.

3. The **two-out play** is a straight double steal, but if the runner attempting to steal second is a sure out, he stops and gets in a rundown play long enough to allow the runner on third to score before the third out is made.

On this play we don't want to draw a pickoff attempt, so the runner takes a short lead. The break to second is normal, and we watch the throw. If the opponent concedes the base, we graciously accept second. We don't tip the play, however, because we may use it later.

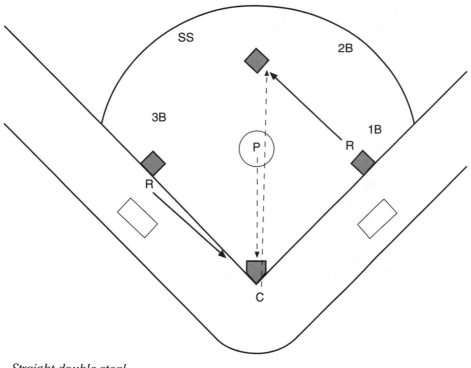

Straight double steal.

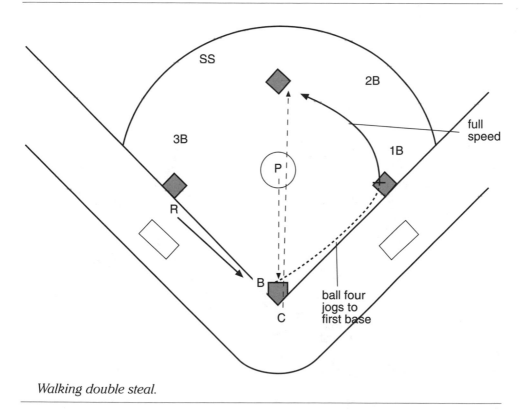

Walking double steal.

4. The **forced-balk play** is normally used in a two-out situation. The runner at first takes a big lead and breaks hard to second when the pitcher goes to the set position. If the pitcher does not balk, then the play automatically becomes the two-out play.

5. The **Oriole sucker play** is a good choice against a left-handed pitcher. The base runners study the pitcher to learn the number of looks he makes to third base. Then, on the pitcher's last look to third base, the runner on third breaks for the plate. At the same time, the runner at first breaks to draw a throw to first base, thereby allowing the runner on third base to steal home.

6. The **oh-shucks play** is another fun play. After the pitcher throws home, the runner at first base breaks to second and falls down. If the catcher throws to first, the runner at third scores. If not, the runner simply returns to first base.

7. The **fake suicide and steal** of second base is used with a below-average runner at first base when the steal is in order. On this play the batter shows the bunt a little early, the runner at third fakes an attempt

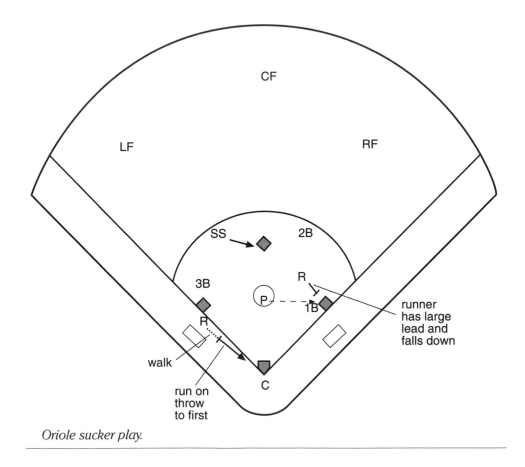

Oriole sucker play.

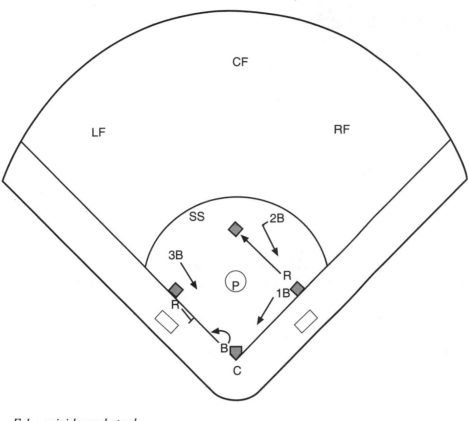

Fake suicide and steal.

to advance on the fake suicide bunt, and the runner at first base steals second while the catcher holds the ball.

8. The **hit-and-run** is one of the worst plays in amateur baseball because it is extremely difficult to execute. It requires great skill by the hitter, who must swing to protect the runner. The runner must run regardless of whether he gets a good lead and a good jump. It is an offensive play that depends on the opposing pitcher to throw a strike. In addition, the offensive team needs to know which middle infielder will be covering second base when the runner breaks.

I don't use it. Furthermore, I believe that every baseball team would be better by not using the hit-and-run. Still, I prefer the hit-and-run to the sacrifice bunt. The purpose is to create action in special pitch-count situations like 1-0, 2-0, and the first pitch. You should anticipate a poor pitch on this play and don't worry about right-field placement. Ask only that the hitter put the ball on the ground.

Running at Second Base

Immediately on returning to the base, the runner checks the outfield depth and positioning, then get the signs from the coach.

• The runner leads off directly toward third base to a distance from which he can always dive back safely, no matter what the defense does. Normally this is a 17-foot lead.

• He uses a shuffle lead as the secondary lead with two slides when he comes off with the pitch.

• The runner should learn to pick up the catcher's signs and know how to call pitches for the hitter. He can then communicate breaking pitches with either verbal or nonverbal methods.

• On fly balls with none out the runner should tag up to advance to third base. With one out the runner should go halfway. Of course, with two outs the runner must run hard to score in case the opponent misses the fly ball.

• Ground-ball advancement rules are used with none or one out. The runner should use this rule of thumb: He should make sure the ball hit to his right goes through the infield before he advances, although on a softly hit ball he can advance if the third baseman fields it. On a ball hit to his left, the runner should be sure it goes past the pitcher before he advances. On a ball hit hard right at him, the runner gets out of the way.

• Finally, on a ground ball with two outs the runner runs hard around third and expects to score because the hitter will beat it out for an infield hit. Scoring from second base on a ground ball is exciting baseball. With two outs, the runner changes his lead at second. Because stealing third is not in order, he gets three steps deep from the base line to create an easier turn when rounding to third.

To steal third, the runner must get a tremendous lead. With oral assistance from the third base coach, the runner can get a good lead. If the coach says, "Plenty of room" or "You're OK," the runner can continue to increase his lead. If the coach says, "Hold it," the runner should take one step back to second and stop. If the coach says, "Back," the runner must quickly get back to second base and be ready to dive. The runner should remember that he is already in scoring position and must never be thrown out while attempting to steal third.

Running at Third Base

The runner at third leads off in foul territory using the three-step lead. He has the right foot in the air when he decides to run or return. He doesn't square the shoulders to home plate.

- When returning to third base after the pitch, the runner should come back in fair territory to block the throw to third. He touches the inside corner of the base.

- To score on ground balls, the runner takes off at the crack of the bat on all batted balls that go down toward the ground. This is the contact play. If the runner is dead out, he should change up and get in a rundown. The runner should look for a wild pitch or passed ball. He must tag on all fly balls and line drives.

Stealing home can be accomplished in two ways. The *straight steal* is a two-out play with less than two strikes. The runner gets a big walking lead and goes on the pitcher's first move. The coach will tell the hitter that the runner is coming so that the hitter takes the pitch. When sliding into home, the runner uses the bent-leg pop-up slide as he touches the near corner. On the front end of *double steal,* the runner should make the ball go past the pitcher when the catcher throws to second.

We use three types of squeeze plays.

1. The first is a suicide squeeze. On this play the runner must be ready to run when the pitcher's front foot plants.
2. Second, we use the safety squeeze. On a safety squeeze the runner makes sure that the ball is on the ground before he runs. The batter is bunting for a hit.
3. Our third play is the shadow squeeze, previously described in the section on bunting.

The goal is to score runs. To score runs, players must always hustle all the way home, regardless of the number of outs. Also, they must be sure to touch all bases. If a player misses a base, he should go back and touch it. The good teams and umpires will always see the misstep. If the team wishes to be champions, they must beat the good teams.

Basic Sliding

Sliding is a falling of the body to the ground in an attempt to elude a tag by a baseman, or a method to slow down and stop at a base. Some runners try to remain standing to slow down. This play can cause stress on the muscles or pulled muscles. Indecision about sliding often results in injury. A good policy is that once the baserunner decides to slide, he slides. He should never change his mind.

Correct sliding requires the player to stay relaxed as he slides without jumping or leaping into the slide. We teach two types of slides—the bent-leg slide, also known as the sitting-standing slide, and the fingers-first slide, also known as the headfirst slide.

Bent-Leg Slide

Bent-leg slide.

In the bent-leg slide the runner slides into the base in an almost sitting position with one leg flexed under the other knee in a figure-4 position. He clenches the fists loosely when sliding to avoid broken fingers. The runner should concentrate on the base for straight-in slides. He must accelerate into the slide to make the slide at full speed. With this slide the runner can remain on the ground or pop up off the ground to continue running the bases. When the runner's extended foot contacts the base in the pop-up slide, the straightening of the bent leg and the momentum of the slide take him to a standing position. The pop-up slide is the most common sliding technique. I recommend the bent-leg pop-up slide on all force plays and at home plate.

Fingers-First Slide

Many people consider the fingers-first slide a dangerous technique. To reduce the risk, limit its use to base stealing. When taking a lead with the intent of stealing a base, the runner should always dive back fingers first. As the runner approaches the base on a steal, he must watch the fielder's glove hand and dive fingers first to avoid the tag. For safety my team does not permit our players to slide fingers first into the catcher.

Most amateur baseball rules currently prohibit the take-out slide, so runners must slide directly into the base and avoid most contact. A deliberate attempt to injure an opponent will not be tolerated. Look for assertive players, not dirty ones.

One of the most exciting aspects of baseball is a daring and hustling team that knows how to run the bases. Speed is a dominant factor in baseball. But alertness, sliding ability, and expert decision making about when to steal or take an extra base present the portrait of the outstanding ball player. Many scouts recognize that the best player on the team is usually the base runner. To accurately track and document the contributions of players, refer to the offensive performace chart.

Fingers-first slide.

General Baserunning Strategies

- Players should always watch the runner directly in front to avoid running up on him.
- The base runner must never allow himself to be doubled up.
- Players should always take into account the wind, the sun, the field, opponents' arms, ballpark outs, the score, and the position of infielders and outfielders.
- The runner should never get picked off at third base, on a hit-and-run play, or on a 3-2 pitch with two out.
- The base runner should know the value of his run and the potential of the hitter.
- A player should avoid being doubled up on popped-up sacrifice bunts or at third base.
- Players should avoid running into tag outs. If a runner cannot avoid a tag, he should run to the glove side to jam the glove into the infielder's chest.
- The first or third out should never be made at third base.
- With two outs the base runner should make the defense throw him out at the plate.
- The runner should not let the infielder block his view when tagging up.
- On rundown plays, the base runner should advance bases. The other runner's job is to stay in the rundown as long as possible to allow others to advance.

About the Author

Bernard P. Walter, Jr., has been the head coach at Arundel High School in Gambrills, Maryland, since 1974. With Coach Walter at the helm, Arundel has won a record-setting nine Maryland State Baseball Championships and was awarded a national title in 1993 by Collegiate Baseball and Easton Sports.

Walter has coached 55 former or current Major Leaguers, including Denny Neagle, Mike Mussina, and John Smoltz. He has been named National High School Baseball Coach of the Year by the National High School Baseball Coaches Association (1993), the National Federation Interscholastic Coaches Association (1996), and the American Baseball Coaches Association (1998), and he's the only baseball coach to have been recog-

© J. Henson/*The Capital Newspaper*

nized by Disney's American Teacher Awards. He was the head coach for the USA Baseball Junior National Team in 1988 and 1990, and he has been a frequent clinician at USA Baseball camps. He also wrote USA Baseball's Coaches Education Program, and he's the educational consultant for MLB Productions' "This Week in Baseball."

Walter holds a bachelor of science in physical education from the University of Maryland at College Park. A member of the American Baseball Coaches Association, he is certified as an athletic administrator with the NIAAA and as a leader level instructor with the NFICEP. In his free time, he enjoys gardening, going to the movies, and spending time with his family. He and his wife, Barbara, are residents of Linthicum, Maryland.

Manufacture more runs on the basepaths!

2001 • 27-minute videotape • ISBN 0-7360-4038-2
(PAL: ISBN 0-7360-4039-0)

Take a trip around the bases like never before! *Bernie Walter's Baserunning Video* provides you with detailed instructions and special tips on this key area of offensive baseball, including

- proper baserunning techniques and strategies,
- tactics to learn before even stepping on the field,
- base-specific guidelines beginning with home plate and progressing around the circuit, and
- special plays to use in first-and-third situations.

Let one of America's most successful baseball coaches show how valuable smart baserunning can be to you and your team. An essential instructional tool, *Bernie Walter's Baserunning Video* will help you create more excitement on the basepaths and more runs on the scoreboard.

HUMAN KINETICS
The Premier Publisher for Sports & Fitness
P.O. Box 5076, Champaign, IL 61825-5076
www.humankinetics.com